Cycling
in
THE HEART
OF ENGLAND

Published by Collins
An imprint of HarperCollins*Publishers*
77–85 Fulham Palace Road
London W6 8JB

www.collins.co.uk
www.bartholomewmaps.com

First published 2002
Copyright © HarperCollins*Publishers* Ltd 2002
Maps © Bartholomew Ltd 2002

Collins® is a registered trade mark of
HarperCollins*Publishers* Limited

Routes compiled by the following:
CTC Shropshire & Mid Wales DA, Helen Gilmour, Gavin Greenlow, Paul Heath,
Dave Hill, Graham Mills, Neil Wheadon

Design by Creative Matters Design Consultancy, Glasgow.
Typeset by Bob Vickers.

Photographs reproduced by kind permission of the following:
Bill Meadows Picture Library pages 11, 19, 22, 32, 47, 51, 74, 89, 101, 103, 107, 114;
Coventry & Warwickshire Promotions page 90; Herefordshire Tourism page 59;
South Warwickshire Tourism page 54; Staffordshire Tourism page 43;
Worcestershire County Council pages 5, 8, 25, 85.

The Publishers welcome comments from readers. Please address your letters to:
Collins Cycling Guides, HarperCollins Cartographic, HarperCollins Publishers,
Westerhill Road, Bishopbriggs, Glasgow, G64 2QT or email cycling@harpercollins.co.uk

Printed in Thailand

ISBN 0 00 712393 0
02/1/12

CONTENTS

KEY TO ROUTES

Route		Grade	Distance km (miles)	Time to allow	Page
1	Stratford-upon-Avon and Wilmcote	moderate	16 (10)	1–3 hours	14
2	Earlswood and Tanworth-in-Arden	moderate	18.5 (11.5)	2–3 hours	17
3	Eccleshall and Cop Mere	moderate	22.5 (14)	2–4 hours	20
4	Droitwich Spa and Hanbury Hall	moderate	27 (17)	2–4 hours	23
5	The Birmingham Main Line Canal	easy	28 (17.5)	2–4 hours	26
6	Shifnal and Ironbridge Gorge	moderate	30 (18.5)	3–5 hours	30
7	Hatton and Packwood	moderate	29.5 (18.5)	2–3 hours	33
8	Hinckley to Bosworth Fields	easy	31.5 (19.5)	2–4 hours	36
9	Tamworth and Twycross	easy	33.5 (21)	2–4 hours	39
10	Cheadle and the Churnet Valley	strenuous	34.5 (21.5)	2–4 hours	42
11	Nantwich and Wrenbury	easy	36 (22.5)	3–4 hours	46
12	Wellington, Longdon upon Tern and High Ercall	easy	43 (27)	2–3 hours	50
13	Bretforton and Stratford-upon-Avon	easy	49.5 (31)	3–6 hours	54
14	The Malverns – Ledbury and Bromyard	moderate	53 (33)	4–5 hours	58
15	Newport and Eccleshall	easy	56 (35)	3–6 hours	62
16	Abbots Bromley and Cannock Chase	strenuous	56 (35)	3–6 hours	66
17	Burton upon Trent and Uttoxeter	moderate	64 (40)	3–6 hours	70
18	Bridgnorth and the Severn Valley	moderate	66.5 (41.5)	4–6 hours	75
19	Stafford and Wedgwood	moderate	72.5 (45)	3–8 hours	80
20	Bewdley and the Wyre Forest	moderate	78.5 (49)	5–7 hours	84
21	Warwick and Rugby	easy	87 (54)	6–9 hours	90
22	Newport and Cannock Chase	moderate	101 (63)	5–7 hours	96
23	Droitwich and the Vale of Evesham	moderate	106 (66)	6–8 hours	102
24	Worcestershire – a grande randonnée	moderate	107 (66.5)	6–8 hours	108
25	Shropshire – a grande randonnée	moderate	113.5 (70.5)	6–9 hours	113

Distances have been rounded up or down to the nearest 0.5km (mile).

Route colour coding

undemanding rides compiled specifically with families in mind
16–32km (10–20 miles)

middle distance rides suitable for all cyclists
32–48km (20–30 miles)

half-day rides for the more experienced and adventurous cyclist
48–64km (30–40 miles)

challenging full-day rides
over 64km (over 40 miles)

grande randonnée – a grand cycling tour
over 100km (60 miles)

 Routes marked with this symbol are off-road or have off-road sections
(includes well-surfaced cycleways as well as rougher off-road tracks)

Malvern Hills

LOCATION MAP

A494 · Wrexham · Nantwich · ⑪ · Stoke-on-Trent · A52 · A46
A525 · A50 · Cheadle · A52 · Nottingham
A5 · ⑩ · A515 · Derby · A607
Llangollen · A495 · A41 · A53 · Stone · M6 · A453 · A606 · Loughborough
Oswestry · A49 · Abbots Bromley · ⑰ Burton upon Trent · A6
A5 · ③ · ⑲ · Stafford · A518 · ⑯
Shrewsbury · ⑮ ㉒ · Newport · Trent · A38 · A444 · A42 · Leicester · A6003
Welshpool · A458 · Wellington · ⑫ · A5 · M42 · A47
Ironbridge · ⑥ · M54 · Tamworth · A5
A458 · ㉕ · Shifnal · ⑨ · ⑧ · M69
WALES · A489 · Bridgnorth · ⑱ · Wolverhampton · Hinckley · A5 · A427
Newtown · Birmingham · M6 · A14 · A14
A489 · ENGLAND · ⑤ · Coventry · A508 · A43
Ludlow · Bewdley · Solihull · M42 · ② · M45 · Northampton
A483 · A456 · ㉔ · A448 · ㉑ ⑦ · Royal Leamington Spa
Builth Wells · A44 · Droitwich · ④ ㉓ ㉔ · Warwick · A45
A44 · Leominster · M5 · Stratford-upon-Avon · A23
Worcester · A442 · ① · M40 · M1
A4112 · A4103 · A44 · A429 · A43 · A5
Hay-on-Wye · A438 · Ledbury · ⑬ · Banbury · A421
A438 · ⑭ · M50 · Evesham · A44
Hereford

KEY TO ROUTE MAPS

M23 (Service area)	Motorway	Cycle route / optional route
A259	'A' road / Dual carriageway	Start of cycle route
B2130	'B' road / Dual carriageway	⑫ Route direction
	Good minor road	B Place of interest
	Minor road	Public house
	Track / bridleway	Café / refreshments
	Railway / station	Restaurant
	Canal / river / lake	Convenience store
	Ferry route	i Tourist Information Centre
50	Contour (height in metres)	P Parking

☎	Telephone
⊼	Picnic site
▲	Camping site
♟	Public toilets
†	Place of worship
☀	Viewpoint
⚑	Golf course
∴	Tumulus
	Urban area
	Woodland

Height above sea level

50	100	150	200	300	400	500	600	700	800	900 metres
165	330	490	655	985	1315	1645	1975	2305	2635	2965 feet

INTRODUCTION

How to use this guide

Collins' *Cycling in the Heart of England* has been devised for those who want trips out on their bicycles along quiet roads and tracks, passing interesting places and convenient refreshment stops without having to devise their own routes. Each of the 25 routes in this book has been compiled and ridden by an experienced cyclist for cyclists of all abilities.

Cycling in the Heart of England is easy to use. Routes range from undemanding rides compiled specifically with families in mind to challenging full-day rides; the type of route is easily identified by colour coding (see page 5). At the start of each route an information box summarises: total distance (in kilometres/miles − distances have been rounded up or down throughout to the nearest 0.5km/mile and are approximate only); grade (easy, moderate or strenuous based on distance and difficulty); terrain; an average time to allow for the route; directions to the start of the route by car and, if appropriate, by train.

Each route is fully mapped and has concise, easy-to-follow directions. Comprehensive information on places of interest and convenient refreshment stops along each route are also given. Accumulated mileages within each route description give an indication of progress, while the profile diagram is a graphic representation of gradients along the route. These should be used as a guide only.

The following abbreviations are used in the route directions:

LHF	left hand fork
RHF	right hand fork
LHS	left hand side
RHS	right hand side
SO	straight on
SP	signpost
TJ	T junction
TL	turn left
TR	turn right
XR	crossroads

Cycling in the Heart of England

The routes are designed to stay away from busy main roads as much as possible, to allow cyclists to discover peaceful back lanes and cycleways, passing all manner of museums, castles and other attractions.

The routes in this book take in the counties of Shropshire, Cheshire, Staffordshire, Leicester-shire, Warwickshire, Worcestershire, Hereford-shire and the city of Birmingham. You will encounter a diverse mix of rural landscapes, picturesque villages, market towns and cities. As well as quiet roads and cycleways, some of the routes follow canal towpaths − the canals were a mainstay of the developing transport system until the advent of the railways.

Sections of the National Cycle Network are used. This is being developed by the charity Sustrans with the help of a £43.5 million grant from the Millennium Commission. The cycle network runs through towns and cities and links urban areas with the countryside. For information write to Sustrans, 35 King Street, Bristol, BSA 4DZ, telephone (0117) 926 8893, or visit their web site at www.sustrans.org.uk

Some of the routes are hilly with steep and undulating sections to be tackled along the way. However, this is compensated for by the spectacular views – and you can always get off and push your bike!

Preparing for a cycling trip

Basic maintenance

A cycle ride is an immense pleasure, particularly on a warm sunny day. Nothing is better than coasting along a country lane gazing over the countryside. Unfortunately, not every cycling day is as perfect as this, and it is important to make sure that your bike is in good order and that you are taking the necessary clothing and supplies with you.

Before you go out on your bicycle check that everything is in order. Pump the tyres up if needed, and check that the brakes are working properly and that nothing is loose – the brakes are the only means of stopping quickly and safely. If there is a problem and you are not sure that you can fix it, take the bike to a cycle repair shop – they can often deal with small repairs very quickly.

When you go out cycling it is important to take either a puncture repair kit or a spare inner tube – it is often quicker to replace the inner

Apple Blossom

tube in the event of a puncture, though it may be a good idea to practise first. You also need a pump, and with a slow puncture the pump may be enough to get you home. To remove the tyre you need a set of tyre levers. Other basic tools are an Allen key and a spanner. Some wheels on modern bikes can be removed by quick release levers built into the bike. Take a lock for your bike and if you have to leave it at any time, leave it in public view and locked through the frame and front wheel to something secure.

What to wear and take with you

It is not necessary to buy specialised cycling clothes. If it is not warm enough to wear shorts wear trousers which are easy to move in but fairly close to the leg below the knee – leggings are ideal – as this stops the trousers catching the chain. If you haven't got narrow-legged trousers, bicycle clips will hold them in. Jeans are not a good idea as they are rather tight and difficult to cycle in, and if they get wet they take a long time to dry. If your shorts or trousers are thin you might get a bit sore from being too long on the saddle. This problem can be reduced by using a gel saddle, and by wearing thicker, or extra, pants. Once you are a committed cyclist you can buy cycling shorts; or undershorts which have a protective pad built in and which can be worn under anything. It is a good idea to wear several thin layers of clothes so that you can add or remove layers as necessary. A zip-fronted top gives easy temperature control. Make sure you have something warm and something waterproof.

If you wear shoes with a firm, flat sole you will be able to exert pressure on the pedals easily, and will have less work to do to make the bicycle move. Gloves not only keep your hands warm but protect them in the event that you come off, and cycling mittens which cushion your hands are not expensive. A helmet is not a legal requirement, but it will protect your head if you fall.

In general it is a good idea to wear bright clothing so that you can be easily seen by motorists, and this is particularly important when it is overcast or getting dark. If you might be out in the dark or twilight fit your bicycle with lights – by law your bicycle must have a reflector. You can also buy reflective bands for your ankles, or to wear over your shoulder and back, and these help motorists to see you.

You may be surprised how quickly you use up energy when cycling, and it is important to eat a carbohydrate meal before you set out. When planning a long ride, eat well the night before. You should eat small amounts of food regularly while you are cycling, or you may find that your energy suddenly disappears, particularly if there are hills or if the weather is cold. It is important to always carry something to eat with you – chocolate, bananas, biscuits – so that if you do start fading away you can restore yourself quickly. In warm weather you will sweat and use up fluid, and you always need to carry something to drink – water will do! Many bicycles have a fitment in which to put a water bottle, and if you don't have one a cycle shop should be able to fit one.

It is also a good idea to carry a small first aid kit. This should include elastoplasts or bandages, sunburn cream, and an anti-histamine in case you are stung by a passing insect.

It is a good idea to have a pannier to carry all these items. Some fit on the handlebars, some to the back of the seat and some onto a back rack. For a day's ride you probably won't need a lot of carrying capacity, but it is better to carry items in a pannier rather than in a rucksack on your back. Pack items that you are carrying carefully – loose items can be dangerous.

Getting to the start of the ride

If you are lucky you will be able to cycle to the start of the ride, but often transport is necessary. If you travel there by train, some sprinter services carry two bicycles without prior booking. Other services carry bicycles free in off-peak periods, but check the details with your local station. Alternatively, you could use your car – it may be possible to get a bike in the back of a hatchback if you take out the front wheel. There are inexpensive, easily fitted car racks which carry bicycles safely. Your local cycle store will be able to supply one to suit you.

Cycling on-road

Cycling on back roads is a delight with quiet lanes, interesting villages and good views. The cycle rides in this book are mainly on quiet roads but you sometimes cross busy roads and have stretches on A and B roads, and whatever sort of road you are on it is essential to ride safely. Always be aware of the possibility or existence of other traffic. Glance behind regularly, signal before you turn or change lane, and keep to the left. If there are motorists around, make sure that they have seen you before you cross their path. Cycling can be dangerous if you are competing for space with motor vehicles, many of which seem to have difficulty in seeing cyclists. When drivers are coming out of side roads, catch their eye before you ride in front of them.

You will find that many roads have potholes and uneven edges. They are much more difficult to spot when you are in a group because of the restricted view ahead, and therefore warnings need to be given. It is a good idea to cycle about a metre out into the road, conditions permitting, so that you avoid the worst of the uneven surfaces and to give you room to move in to the left if you are closely overtaken by a motor vehicle.

Other things to be careful of are slippery roads, particularly where there is mud or fallen leaves. Sudden rain after a period of dry weather often makes the roads extremely slippery. Dogs, too, are a hazard because they often move unpredictably, and sometimes like to chase cyclists. If you are not happy, stop or go slowly until the problem has passed.

Pedalling

Many modern bikes have 18 or 21 gears with three rings at the front and six or seven on the back wheel, and for much of the time you will find that the middle gear at the front with the range of gears at the back will be fine. Use your gears to find one that is easy to pedal along in so that your feet move round easily and you do not put too much pressure on your knees. If you are new to the bike and the gears it is a good idea to practise changing the gears on a stretch of flat, quiet road so that when you need to change gears quickly you will be ready to do so.

Cycling in a group

When cycling in a group it is essential to do so in a disciplined manner for your own, and others', safety. Do not ride too close to the bicycle in front of you – keep about a bicycle's length between you so that you will have space to brake or stop. Always keep both hands on the handlebars, except when signalling, etc. It is alright to cycle two abreast on quiet roads, but if it is necessary to change from cycling two abreast to single file this is usually done by the outside rider falling in behind the nearside rider; always cycle in single file where there are double white lines, on busy roads, or on

The SVR in Shropshire Highly Station

narrow and winding roads where you have a restricted view of the road ahead. Overtake on the right (outside) only; do not overtake on the inside.

It is important to pass information to other members of the group, for example:

car up – a vehicle is coming up behind the group and will be overtaking;

car down – a vehicle is coming towards the group;

single up – get into single file;

stopping – stopping, or

slowing/easy – slowing due to junction, etc., ahead;

on the left – there is an obstacle on the left, e.g. pedestrian, parked car;

pothole – pothole (and point towards it).

Accidents

In case of an accident, stay calm and, if needed, ring the emergency services on 999. It is a good idea to carry a basic first aid kit and perhaps also one of the commercial foil wraps to put around anyone who has an accident to keep them warm. If someone comes off their bicycle move them and the bike off the road if it is safe to do so. Get someone in the party to warn approaching traffic to slow down, and if necessary ring for an ambulance.

Cycling off-road

All the routes in this book take you along legal rights of way – bridleways, byways open to all traffic and roads used as public paths – it is illegal to cycle along footpaths. Generally the off-road sections of the routes will be easy if the weather and ground are dry. If the weather has been wet and the ground is muddy, it is not a good idea to cycle along bridleways unless you do not mind getting dirty and unless you have a mountain bike which will not get blocked up with mud. In dry weather any bicycle will be able to cover the bridleway sections, but you may need to dismount if the path is very uneven.

Off-road cycling is different to cycling on the road. The average speed is lower, you will use more energy, your riding style will be different and there is a different set of rules to obey – the off-road code:

1 Give way to horse riders and pedestrians, and use a bell or call out to warn someone of your presence.

2 Take your rubbish with you.

3 Do not light fires.

4 Close gates behind you.

5 Do not interfere with wildlife, plants or trees.

6 Use only tracks where you have a right of way, or where the landowner has given you permission to ride.

7 Avoid back wheel skids, which can start erosion gulleys and ruin the bridleway.

Some of the off-road rides take you some miles from shelter and civilisation – take waterproofs, plenty of food and drink and basic tools – especially spare inner tubes and tyre repair equipment. Tell someone where you are going and approximately when you are due back. You are more likely to tumble off your bike riding off-road, so you should consider wearing a helmet and mittens with padded palms.

Useful contacts

Cycling organisations
CTC – see page 119
Sustrans – see page 8

Cycling websites
Online resources for cyclists in the UK
www.cyclecafe.com

Internet bicycling hub
www.cyclery.com

Information and support for cyclists in the UK
www.cycleweb.co.uk

Cycling information station
www.cycling.uk.com

Local cycle hire
Back on Track
Unit 2
No 6 North Malvern Road
Malvern
Worcestershire
Telephone (01684) 565777

Lutterworth Cycle Centre
Leicester Road
Leicester
Telephone (01455) 559309

Parker International
Lillyhurst Industrial Estate
Abbey Road
Sheriffhales
Shropshire
Telephone (01952) 676777

Cycles & Tandems
1 Stourbridge Road
Halesowen
West Midlands
Telephone (0121) 550 7335

Local cycle shops
C R Cycles
89 Tape Street
Cheadle
Telephone (01538) 752145

Just Bikes
40 Market Street
Telford
Telephone (01952) 246625

Pauls Pedals
23 Whitburn Street
Bridgnorth
Telephone (01746) 768792

Aztec Cycles
44 Foregate Street
Stafford
Telephone (01785) 607511

Bikes and Kites
1 Lock Cottage
Burton On Trent
Telephone (01283) 790070

B & V Wirdman Cycles
40 West Street
Warwick
Telephone (01926) 492886

Briley Cycles
16 Wood Street
Stratford-upon-Avon
Telephone (01789) 292906

Warwick Cycles
20 West Street
Warwick
Telephone (0926) 410358

D & I Leisure
10b Comberton Hill
Kidderminster
Telephone (01562) 741300

Vale Cycles
23 Port Street
Evesham
Telephone (01386) 41204

J H Cycles
846 Alum Rock Road
Birmingham
Telephone (0121) 328 6262

Tourist Information
Heart of England Tourist Board
Telephone (01905) 763436
www.visitheartofengland.com

Birmingham Convention & Visitor Centre
Telephone (0121) 643 2514

Derby Tourist Information Centre
Telephone (01332) 255802

Hereford Tourist Information Centre
Telephone (01432) 268430

Shrewsbury Tourist Information Centre
Telephone (01743) 281200

Stafford Tourist Information Centre
Telephone (01785) 619619

Warwick Tourist Information Centre
Telephone (01926) 492212

Worcester Tourist Information Centre
Telephone (01905) 726311

Local councils
Birmingham County Council
Telephone (0121) 303 7485
www.birmingham.gov.uk

Derbyshire County Council
Telephone (01629) 580000
www.derbyshire.gov.uk

Hereford County Council
Telephone (01432) 260000
www.herefordshire.gov.uk

Leicestershire County Council
Telephone (0116) 232 3232
www.leicestershire.gov.uk

Shropshire County Council
Telephone (01743) 251000
www.shropshire-cc.gov.uk

Staffordshire County Council
Telephone (01785) 223121
www.staffordshire.gov.uk

Warwickshire County Council
Telephone (0845) 090 7000
www.warwickshire.gov.uk

Worcestershire County Council
Telephone (01905) 763763
www.worcestershire.gov.uk

Travel by rail
National rail enquiries
Telephone (08457) 484950

Railtrack
www.railtrack.com

The Train Line
www.thetrainline.com

Weather forecasts
BBC Weather
www.bbc.co.uk/weather

The Met. Office
Telephone (09003) 406 108
www.met-office.gov.uk

UK Weather Links
www.ukweather.links.co.uk

Youth Hostels Association of England and Wales
Telephone (01727) 855215
www.yha.org.uk

STRATFORD-UPON-AVON AND WILMCOTE

Route information

Distance 16km (10 miles)

Grade Moderate

Terrain A wide variety of terrain – grassy bridleway, stony bridleway (uphill), canal towpath, quiet roads and two short sections of A road (care required, especially along the A46).

Time to allow 1–3 hours.

Getting there by car Stratford-upon-Avon is 12.5km (8 miles) south west of Warwick on the A3400 and A422. There is a pay and display car park at the cattle market, close to the start of the route at the railway station.

Getting there by train There is a regular service to Stratford-upon-Avon Station. For travel information telephone (08457) 484950 or visit www.nationalrail.co.uk

From Stratford-upon-Avon the route heads north through residential areas to reach a bridleway leading into Welcombe Park. From this vantage point you can admire the views and the obelisk erected to a local industrialist and parliamentarian of the 19th century. Descending to tarmac, and turning west to Wilmcote, the rest of the route is mostly along quiet roads, apart from the two very short sections of A road. The return to Stratford is alongside the scenic Stratford-upon-Avon Canal.

Route description

Exit Stratford railway station and TL at TJ (effectively SO), no SP. Head towards town centre and at first set of traffic lights:

1 TL at XR into Arden Street, no SP.

2 SO at XR into Clapton Road, no SP. Cross canal and continue into residential area.

3 TR into Blue Cap Road, no SP. At top of road, bear left in front of SP Blue Cap Road. At end of this short stretch of road, follow tarmac climbing gently.

4 SO through gate. Pass Welcombe Park reservoir on RHS. Climb obvious bridleway. At the top, pass through gate and continue SO, keeping woods on RHS and open field on LHS. Shortly afterwards TR at TJ of bridleways, pass through gate and head towards obelisk. Follow bridleway as it passes to L of obelisk, head for nearest group of red buildings to pass through gate (buildings on RHS) and descend track. Arrive TJ with road:

5 TL at TJ, no SP (post box 20m along road on RHS). Pass golf club on LHS. At top of hill:

6 TL into Kings Lane, SP (A46) West, along Kings Lane.

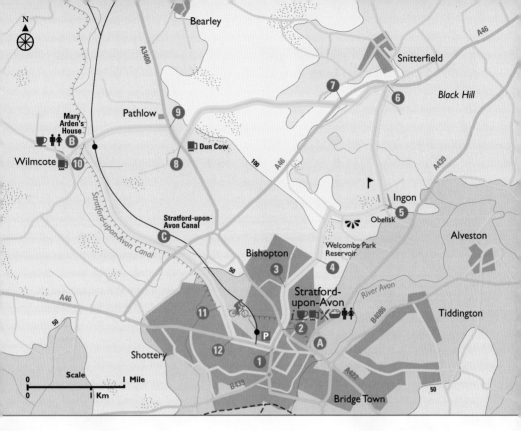

7 TL at TJ, SP Stratford/Wilmcote (7km/ 4.5 miles). Take CARE along this road for 30m and TR, SP Wilmcote.

8 TR at TJ onto A3400, SP Wilmcote.

9 TL, SP Wilmcote/Mary Arden's House. Just after crossing railway bridge:

10 To visit Mary Arden's House, SO.

To continue main route, TL onto cycle path, no SP (bridge over canal is metal railed). Cycle alongside Stratford-upon-Avon canal. Immediately after passing under bridge 64:

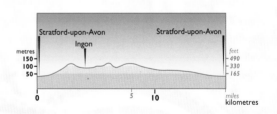

11 TL up ramp, no SP. TL at TJ, no SP, and again TL at TJ, SP 5 (next to Timothy's Bridge Road).

12 TL at TJ, SP 5, cross roundabout and return to station to finish the ride.

16km (10 miles)

Places of interest along the route

A Stratford-upon-Avon

Famed as the birthplace of William Shakespeare, tourism has been established in the town for a long time – the first big celebrations in Shakespeare's honour were organised in 1789. The many attractions include **Shakespeare's Birthplace and Exhibition**, Henley Street, which gives the visitor an insight into life when Shakespeare was a child. Open mid-March to mid-October, Monday–Saturday 0900–1700, Sunday 0930–1700; mid-October to mid-March, Monday–Saturday 0930–1600, Sunday 1000–1600. On the banks of the River Avon, **Cox's Yard** was formerly the site of an historic timber yard. Old buildings have been restored to blend with new. Inside there are shops and a café, restaurant and pub which serves beer brewed on site. The yard is open all year, daily 0900–2300. Admission free. Also in Cox's yard is **The Stratford Tales** which explores the sights and sounds of Stratford through the ages. Charge. As well as performing the works of Shakespeare, the **Royal Shakespeare Company** offers tours which give a glimpse of the working life of the company. Open all year, Monday–Saturday from 0930, Sunday from 1130. Charge. There are lots of other attractions to visit in and around Stratford. Contact the Tourist Information Centre on (01789) 293127 or visit www.stratford-upon-avon.co.uk

B Mary Arden's House, Wilmcote

The house belonged to Robert Arden, Shakespeare's grandfather, and was the childhood home of Mary Arden, Shakespeare's mother. The house is furnished as the home of a yeoman farmer and the associated buildings illustrate rural life. Café. Open all year, summer Monday–Saturday 0930–1700, Sunday 1000–1700; winter Monday–Saturday 1000–1600, Sunday 1030–1600. Telephone (01789) 293455 or visit www.shakespeare. org.uk

C Stratford-upon-Avon Canal

At 26 miles long the Stratford-upon-Avon Canal links Stratford and the River Avon to the Worcester and Birmingham Canal at King's Norton. It took 21 years to complete from the initial Act of Parliament in 1793. By the 1950s only the occasional working boat was using the northern section of the canal and closure was recommended. Public protest was the start of a massive campaign to save the canal and it was reopened in 1964, after much hard work by volunteers, prison labourers, army units and National Trust staff. Today the canal is operated by British Waterways. There is free access to the section of canal used in this route, but much of the rest of the canal is not accessible to bicycles due to the condition of the towpaths. For more information contact British Waterways on (01923) 201120 or visit www.britishwaterways.co.uk

Food and drink

There is plenty of choice in Stratford and two pubs in Wilmcote, both of which serve bar meals.

Dun Cow, Pathlow
Real ales, bar meals and outside seating.

EARLSWOOD AND TANWORTH-IN-ARDEN

Route information

 Distance 18.5km (11.5 miles)

 Grade Moderate

 Terrain Tarmac roads throughout – quiet lanes and one section of B road.

Time to allow 2–3 hours.

 Getting there by car Earlswood is 6.5km (4 miles) south west of Solihull, just north of the M42, junction 3. There is a small free car park at the railway station, the start of the route.

 Getting there by train There is a regular service to Earlswood. For travel information telephone (08457) 484950 or visit www.nationalrail.co.uk

Starting from Earlswood station, the route heads south towards Tanworth-in-Arden, passing many of the lovely homes associated with south Birmingham's commuter belt. The ride passes the entrance to a farm park before passing the private stately residence at Umberslade. The B4101 (care required along here) leads to an attractive view across a pair of reservoirs at Earlswood, where you could picnic, eat in a pub or enjoy a tea stop at the craft centre before returning to the station.

Places of interest along the route

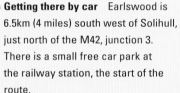 **Umberslade Children's Farm, Tanworth-in-Arden**

Situated in 526ha (1300 acres) of farmland, Umberslade Children's Farm is a working farm. All the usual favourites such as pigs, calves, goats and shire horses are present, with the addition of ferret racing and pony and donkey rides around the farm. There is also an adventure play area. Café and farm shop. Open 1000–1700, daily through Easter, summer and autumn school holidays; also every weekend, March to early November. Charge. Telephone (01564) 742251; www.umbersladefarm.co.uk

B Manor Farm Craft Centre, Earlswood

A small selection of units make up Manor Farm Craft Centre. There are a variety of craft shops, a riding stables and a café sited around a courtyard on this working farm. Open all year, Tuesday–Sunday and Bank Holiday Monday 0900–1700. Telephone (01564) 702729.

Food and drink

Earlswood has a store and a pub and there are stores and a pub at Tanworth-in-Arden. Refreshments are also available at Umberslade Children's Farm and Manor Farm Craft Centre.

 Café, Earlswood Industrial Estate
Open 1000–1400.

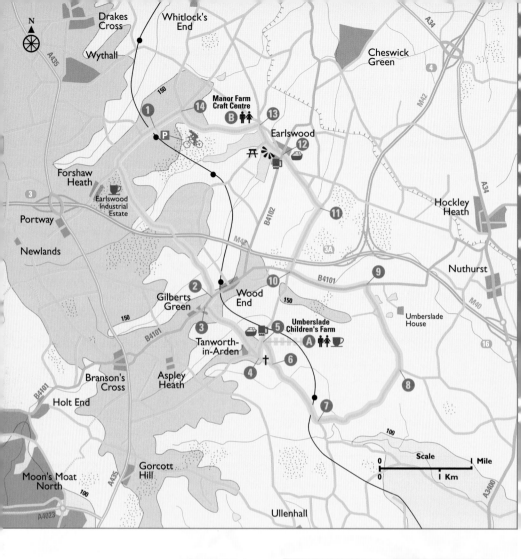

Route description 🚴

Start from station car park, and head towards exit.

1 TL at TJ, no SP, and cross railway. Cross M42 to pass numerous large houses set back from the road in pretty gardens.

2 TR at TJ onto B4101, SP Redditch/ Tanworth.

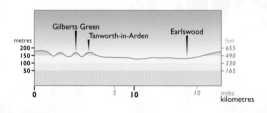

3 TL, SP Tanworth, then immediately TL at TJ, no SP (opposite Redwood Lodge). Enter Tanworth-in-Arden. In front of the church:

4 TL along The Green, no SP. Pass village stores and Bell Inn on LHS.

5 To visit Umberslade Children's Farm, follow SP.

Otherwise, to continue route, TR into Butts Lane, SP Danzey Green/Henley.

6 TL at TJ opposite wooden bench, no SP. Descend, passing weak bridge on LHS. Cross bridge and:

7 TL into Pig Trot Lane, no SP.

8km (5 miles)

Tanworth-in-Arden

8 TL at TJ, SP Earlswood. Pass Umberslade House on RHS.

9 TL at TJ onto B4101, SP Tanworth/ Earlswood. Take CARE on this road.

10 TR at XR into Tithe Barn Lane, no SP.

11 TL, SP Earlswood.

12 SO at XR, SP Wythall. Descend and TL, no SP, along a raised, narrow road next to reservoir. Pass around metal rails to continue SO (single reservoir on LHS). Rejoin main road.

13 TL at XR, SP Manor Farm Craft Centre (16km/10 miles). Pass craft centre on RHS.

14 TL at TJ into Rumbush Lane, SP Earlswood Station/Foreshaw Heath. Return to station car park to finish the ride. *18.5km (11.5 miles)*

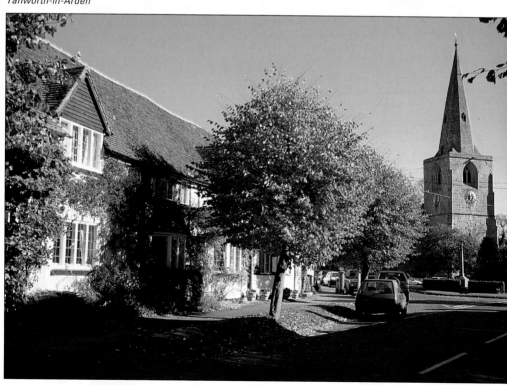

ECCLESHALL AND COP MERE

Route information

Distance 22.5km (14 miles)

Grade Moderate

Terrain Mostly quiet lanes through farmland and a short stretch of B road into Eccleshall.

Time to allow 2–4 hours.

Getting there by car Norton Bridge is 4.5km (3 miles) south west of Stone, off the B5026. Park at the railway station, the start of the route.

Getting there by train There is a regular service to Norton Bridge. For travel information telephone (08457) 484950 or visit www.nationalrail.co.uk

A pleasant figure-of-eight route, with expansive views across the Staffordshire countryside. Starting from Norton Bridge the route heads west to Eccleshall and onto Offleyhay, before turning north east and then east for the return journey. The route passes Cop Mere, a Site of Special Scientific Interest, and Offleyhay Mill Pond, where plenty of wildfowl can usually be seen. It is possible to stop in Eccleshall on the way out and call at the Bird of Prey Centre on the way back.

Route description

TR out of Norton Bridge railway station car park. Cycle through Norton Bridge, passing Railway pub on LHS.

1 TL at TJ, SP Eccleshall. SO at XR, SP Eccleshall. Pass Fletchers Garden Centre on LHS as you enter Eccleshall.

2 SO at mini roundabout in Eccleshall, into High Street, SP Loggerheads (Teazells Tearooms on LHS). Pass Royal Oak pub on L and continue past church.

3 TL, SP Elford Heath, and climb.

4 TR at XR, SP Cop Mere, and continue to Cop Mere.

5 SO at XR by Cop Mere, SP Cheswardine (8km/5 miles). Views of mere on RHS. Continue along this road, passing picnic site on LHS.

6 TR, SP Croxton (Offleyhay mill pond on LHS), and climb.

7 SO at XR, SP Brockton. Continue for descent and good views, passing Sugnall Tearooms on LHS before TJ.

8 TR at TJ, no SP. *13.5km (8.5 miles)*

9 TR at TJ over A519 and immediately TL, SP Norton Bridge.

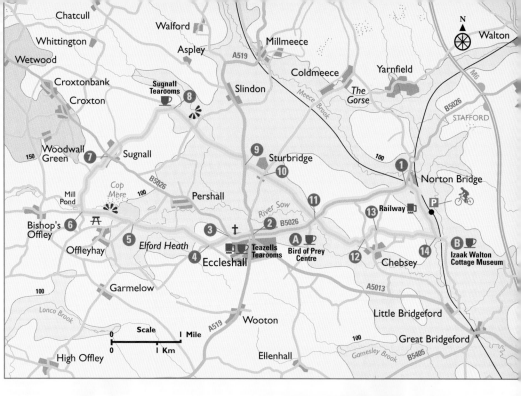

10 SO at XR, SP Chebsey. **16km (10 miles)**

11 To visit the Bird of Prey Centre, TR at XR.

To continue main route, SO at XR, SP Chebsey
(crossing outward route).

12 TL at grass triangle, SP Norton
Bridge.

13 SO at XR, no SP. **20km (12.5 miles)**

14 TL at TJ, SP Norton Bridge. To visit
Izaak Walton Cottage Museum, TR at TJ for
0.5km (0.3 mile).

Otherwise, continue along this road and TR
into station car park to finish the ride.

22.5km (14 miles)

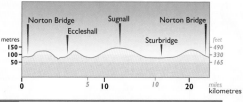

Food and drink

*There are several opportunities for
refreshment along the route. There is a
pub in Eccleshall and refreshments are
available at Fletchers Garden Centre.*

 Railway Pub, Norton Bridge
Families are welcome here.

Teazells Tearooms, Eccleshall
Light snacks and meals served.

Sugnall Tearooms, Little Sugnall
Open Monday–Friday only.

A Bird of Prey Centre, Fletchers Country Garden Centre, Eccleshall

Captive bred birds are displayed here to raise money to help injured birds. The birds were originally taken in by the Gentleshaw Bird of Prey Hospital. After regaining full health birds capable of surviving are released back into the wild. Birds which are permanently disabled but have a good quality of life are paired and the resulting offspring are eventually released back into the wild. The centre offers bird handling courses and flying displays. Café in the garden centre. Telephone (01785) 850379 to confirm opening times.

B Izaak Walton Cottage Museum, Norton Bridge

Izaak Walton wrote *The Compleat Angler* in 1653. The cottage was eventually left to Stafford Corporation and is now restored and open to the public. It is a typical mid-Staffordshire, timber framed building with wattle and daub infill and is now home to a small library containing a first edition copy of *The Compleat Angler*. A museum describes Walton's life and contains a variety of fishing collections. Herb garden and picnic area. Open April to October, Tuesday–Sunday and Bank Holiday Mondays 1100–1630; November and March, weekends 1100–1600. Charge. Telephone (01785) 619619.

Droitwich Spa (see route 4)

Route information

 Distance 27km (17 miles)

Grade Moderate

Terrain Mostly flat, quiet lanes, with one stretch along a reasonably quiet B road and one climb up to Hanbury Hall.

Time to allow 2–4 hours.

Getting there by car Droitwich is 9.5km (6 miles) north east of Worcester on the A38. There are several car parks in Droitwich. Use the one by St Andrews shopping centre/Victoria Square, close to the Tourist Information Centre (TIC) and the start of the route.

Getting there by train There is a railway station at Droitwich. For travel information telephone (08457) 484950 or visit www.nationalrail.co.uk

From the spa town of Droitwich the route heads east to Hanbury, often used as a real-life version of Ambridge, the fictional town featured in The Archers. *From here the route turns south, crossing a ford, and then west for the return back to Droitwich.*

Places of interest along the route

Ⓐ Droitwich Spa
Droitwich has been a centre for the salt industry since before Roman times and by the 11th century the town was an important industrial and commercial centre. Today Droitwich is a pleasant market town. In 1934 a huge radio transmitter was erected near Droitwich and there is a recreated radio studio in the TIC. The first brine baths were constructed in the 19th century and there is still a therapeutic spa in operation – the density of salt in the water makes floating in the brine similar to swimming in the Dead Sea! Contact the TIC for more information on (01905) 774312.

Ⓑ Hanbury Hall, Hanbury
A William and Mary style house built in 1701 with beautifully decorated interiors. The grounds feature a recreated 18th-century garden and parkland. Tearoom. National Trust property. Open April to October, Sunday–Wednesday 1330–1730; garden and tearoom open 1200–1700. Charge. Telephone (01527) 821214; www.nationaltrust.org.uk

Ⓒ Hanbury
The site of pre-historic earthworks, Hanbury grew up around a nunnery, founded in the first century AD. Although nothing remains of the nunnery, the village church, St Werburgh's, is centuries old and much rebuilt over the centuries. The Jinny Ring Craft Centre houses individual craft studios and has landscaped gardens and water features. Tearoom. Open all year, Tuesday–Saturday 1030–1700, Sunday and Bank Holidays opens 1100. Admission free. Telephone (01527) 821272; www.jinneyringcraft.co.uk

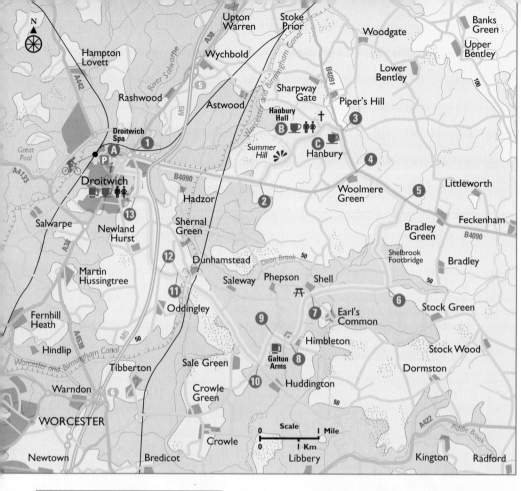

Route description

To start from Droitwich railway station, exit station into Omberlsey Way and head east to town centre. Cross The Saltway and follow SP to TIC (Victoria Square).

To start route from TIC, cycle north east along St Andrews Street. TR into High Street. TL at TJ into Queen Street, SP Bromsgrove/A38.

1 TR at XR (traffic lights), SP Alcester/B4090. SO at next two mini roundabouts. Cross Worcester and Birmingham Canal.

2 TL, SP Hanbury Hall (good views of hall on LHS), and pass entrance to hall on LHS. Gradually climb towards Hanbury. To visit Hanbury Church, TL, SP Hanbury Church. Continue into Hanbury village. **8km (5 miles)**

3 TR at XR, SP Redditch (Jinny Ring Craft Centre on RHS). Descend.

4 TL at TJ, SP Alcester/B4090 (9km/5.5 miles). Continue along B4090. At top of rise:

5 TR into Hollowfields Road, SP Ford. Continue to ford and cross Shellbrook via Shellbrook Footbridge (entrance on RHS, 5m before ford).

6 TR at TJ, SP Himbleton.

7 SO at XR, SP Himbleton (16km/10 miles). Pass Shellbrook picnic site on RHS.

8 TR at TJ, SP Crowle. Continue into Himbleton, past Galton Arms.

9 TL at TJ, SP Crowle.

10 TR at XR, SP Droitwich. Cross railway and canal.

11 TL, SP Droitwich (22.5km/14 miles).

12 TR at TJ, SP Droitwich. Pass under M5 motorway. Continue into outskirts of Droitwich. Take third exit at roundabout, no SP.
24km (15 miles)

13 Take third exit at roundabout, no SP. Descend (Tagwell Road). TR at TJ into Worcester Road. Descend to mini roundabout where SO. TL into St Andrews and finish ride by TIC.
27km (17 miles)

Food and drink

Plenty of choice in Droitwich. Refreshments are also available at Hanbury Hall and the Jinny Ring Craft Centre.

Galton Arms, Himbleton
Bar meals served at lunchtime.

Hanbury Hall

Route information

 Distance 28km (17.5 miles)

Grade Easy

Terrain One short stretch of A road but the remainder of the route is off-road cycling along canal tow-paths. The surfaces include tarmac, brick, fine gravel, cinders and short stretches of soil – take great care during wet weather. There is an open unlit tunnel, where lights will be useful.

 Time to allow 2–4 hours (allow extra time to visit the places of interest).

Getting there by car There are several car parks in Birmingham city centre, west of New Street Station, the start of the route.

Getting there by train Birmingham is well served by trains from all parts of the UK. For travel information telephone (08457) 484950 or visit www.nationalrail.co.uk

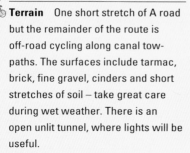

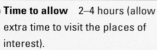

This route is an almost entirely traffic-free journey through one of the most built-up industrial centres of the country. After a short section of road in Birmingham, the route joins the Birmingham Main Line Canal at Gas Street Basin. The first couple of miles along the canal run through industrial surroundings but for most of the route it is easy to forget that you are in the centre of a huge conurbation. Half way to Wolverhampton, the route leaves the Main Line to visit the Black Country Museum returning to pass though Cosely Tunnel to arrive at Broad Street Basin in Wolverhampton. The return to Birmingham can either be by reversing the route along the canal or by taking the train from Wolverhampton. There are other railway stations along the route at which the journey can be cut short. Much of the towpath is part of the National Cycle Network (Birmingham Cycle Route 5/Birmingham and Black Country Canal Cycleway).

Places of interest along the route

A Birmingham

Gas Street Basin is at the junction of the Worcester and Birmingham Canal and the Birmingham Canal. Worcester Bar is the strip of land which was originally required to ensure that the Birmingham Canal did not lose water to the new Worcester and Birmingham Canal, and to make it more difficult for through traffic on the Worcester and Birmingham Canal. **Brindley Place** has recently been developed from derelict canalside land to a thriving centre complete with a wide variety of pubs, restaurants and shops, and the **Sea Life Centre**. The centre is home to over 55 displays, including the world's first completely transparent underwater tunnel. Café and gift shop. Open all year, daily 1000–1700. Charge. Telephone (0121) 643 6777. For more information on Birmingham, contact the Tourist Information Centre on (0121) 643 2514 or visit www.birmingham.gov.uk

B Black Country Museum and Dudley Zoo and Castle, Dudley

The **Black Country Museum** is a collection of historic buildings brought from all around the Black Country, creating an opportunity to experience life in the industrial heart of Britain. Situated on the Tipton Branch of the Main Line Canal, there is an underground coal mine, and tram rides, shops, houses, a pub and a school to visit. Many traditional crafts are demonstrated. Café, pub and 1930s fried fish shop. Open March to October, daily 1000–1700; November to February, Wednesday–Sunday 1000–1600. Charge. Telephone (0121) 557 9643; www.bclm. co.uk. The adjacent **Dudley Zoo and Castle** is an alternative attraction. The zoo has been established for over 60 years and as well as being heavily involved in conservation, is home to over 200 species of animals. Dudley Castle was originally built in 1070 and extensively rebuilt in 1530. It was in use until 1750, when it was gutted by a huge fire. A visitor centre describes the castle's history. Café and picnic areas. Open daily, summer 1000–1630; winter 1000–1530. Charge. Telephone (01384) 215313, www.dudleyzoo.org.uk.

C Birmingham Main Line Canal

Work on a canal between Birmingham and Wolverhampton was started in 1768 by James Brindley and completed in 1772 with the main canal 37km (23 miles) long. The canal was heavily modified by Thomas Telford after 1824. The new Main Line at Smethwick (followed by this ride) was added to bypass a rise and fall of six locks which had caused delays and water supply problems. Telford's main improvements were in straightening and improving the towpaths and it is his work which gives the cyclist such a pleasant, flat route though the industrial heartlands. Contact British Waterways for more information on (01923) 201120; www.britishwaterways.co.uk

Route description

Start from Birmingham New Street station. Leave by Victoria Square exit (much quieter and more suitable for cycles than the main exit, although no lifts are available).

1 TL onto Navigation Street and SO at traffic lights. Join RHS pavement outside Brunel Street car park (part of Birmingham Cycle Route 5).

2 TR under bridge, SP Cycle Route 5/ Convention Centre. At top of rise re-join road and TL along Holliday Street, SP Cycle Route 5.

3 TR into Bridge Street, SP Cycle Route 5. As you reach crest of rise, TL at small square giving access to the canal basin outside James Brindley pub. This is Gas Street Basin. Descend ramp to R and join RHS towpath. Pass through Broad Street tunnel (actually a number of bridges connected together), under The Merchant Stores pub and pass International Convention Centre on RHS.

4 TL outside National Indoor Arena, SP Olympian Suite/Sea Life Centre. Drop down to towpath level again. You are now cycling alongside the Birmingham Main Line Canal to Wolverhampton

5 SO at Rotton Park Junction, SP Wolverhampton. At next footbridge, cross to LHS towpath (the cycle route changes side from time to time to take the best surfaced towpath). Continue to pass Winson Green junction.

6 Immediately after Winson Green junction, cross back to RHS towpath. *5km (3 miles)*

7 At Smethwick Junction, the Old (original) Line deviates to R of Main Line – continue along RHS towpath of Main Line Canal (there is an informative SP here describing this section

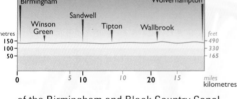

of the Birmingham and Black Country Canal Cycleway).

---

8 Arrive Bromford Junction. Cross canal to LHS towpath. **9km (5.5 miles)**

9 At Dudley Port Junction, cross canal to RHS towpath.

10 Pass Tipton Station (13.5km/8.5 miles), accessible to R of canal (catch train back to Birmingham to shorten ride).

11 Arrive Factory Bridge (Barge and Barrel pub on RHS). To visit Black Country Museum/Dudley Zoo/Dudley Castle, double back and cross footbridge to go down

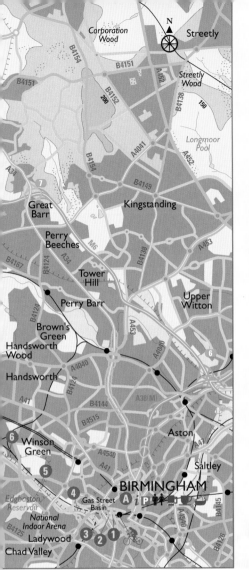

A4037, SP Black Country Museum. The entrance to the museum is on RHS (16km/ 10 miles). After visit retrace route to Factory Bridge and rejoin Main Line canal, where TL towards Wolverhampton.

Otherwise, continue along Main Line towpath towards Wolverhampton.

12 Take care passing through Cosely Tunnel (330m long and DARK). Fortunately towpath is fitted with hand rail to prevent early baths. Continue to pass Horsley Fields Bridge.

13 Just after Horsley Fields Bridge, climb to cross a canal branch and return to towpath, SP Cycle Path/Town Centre. **25.5km (16 miles)**

14 Pass under Broad Street Bridge into Broad Street Basin. TR to join cycle path running along main road and head towards traffic lights. TL at traffic lights (cycle crossing) and follow cycle path along LHS of ring road (St Davids). Pass under next bridge and follow path to L to reach Wolverhampton Station.

28km (17.5 miles)

Tipton Branch which leaves Main Line Canal here.

a TL at Tipton Junction (no choice) and cross to opposite towpath at next foot bridge, SP Cycle Path/Black County Living Museum. Arrive back at Tipton Junction, TL again and continue along Tipton Branch towards Dudley Tunnel.

b Before road bridge and large pipe, TL up path to join main road. TR at traffic lights onto

Food and drink

There is a huge choice of eating places close to New Street Station. There are pubs and restaurants spread along the first 1km (0.6 mile) of the canal but after this there are no eating places until the Barge and Barrel and the Fountain Inn. Refreshments are available at the Black Country Museum, Dudley Zoo and in Wolverhampton.

Barge and Barrel, Tipton
Bar meals at lunchtimes.

Fountain Inn
Half-way along the Tipton Branch. Bar meals available.

SHIFNAL AND IRONBRIDGE GORGE

Route information

Distance 30km (18.5 miles)

Grade Moderate

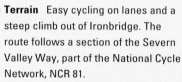

Terrain Easy cycling on lanes and a steep climb out of Ironbridge. The route follows a section of the Severn Valley Way, part of the National Cycle Network, NCR 81.

Time to allow 3–5 hours.

Getting there by car Shifnal is 11km (7 miles) south of Newport on the A464 and A4169. Park in the town's main car park in the centre of town, near the railway station.

Getting there by train There is a regular rail service to Shifnal. Telephone (08457) 484950; www.national rail.co.uk for travel information.

A route offering good views across Shropshire and lots to see and do in Ironbridge. From Shifnal the route makes a figure-of-eight as far as Brockton, from where cyclists can head to Ironbridge and the River Severn, or return to Shifnal, avoiding a steep climb (total distance 17.5km/11 miles).

Route description

If starting from Shifnal railway station, TR out of station and keep right as road becomes Stanton Road.

To start from the car park, TL into Aston Street and keep right as road becomes Stanton Road.

1 TR, SP Industrial Estate. Bear right and climb over bridge.

2 TR at TJ, no SP (1.5km/1 mile). SO over A464 at XR, SP Ryton.

3 TL at TJ, no SP. Continue on this road, passing interesting private house on RHS which was Hinkesmans Spring Brewery. Pass red sandstone cliff on RHS and cross River Worfe. Climb to TJ.

4 TR at TJ, SP Kemberton. Then take first TL, no SP.

5 TR at XR, no SP, and gently climb for panoramic views.

6 TR at TJ, SP Shifnal B4379.

9.5km (6 miles)

7 To return to Shifnal, continue SO, SP Shifnal, to direction 16.

To visit Ironbridge Gorge, TL, SP Coalport.

8 SO at XR across A442, SP Coalport. Gradually climb, enjoying wide ranging views from summit (11.5km/7 miles). Descend steeply (CARE) into Coalport. SO over River Severn (Woodbridge Inn on LHS).

9 TR, opposite pub, SP Cycle Route 81/ Severn Valley Way. Descend steps onto cycle route and follow cycle route past Maws Craft Centre on R. Continue as cycle route joins road, and passes Jackfield Tile Museum on LHS.

10 TR at TJ, SP Cycle Route 81. TL at Jackfield Sidings (by old level crossing gates), SP Cycle Route 81. Continue along cycleway through Bridge Car Park. *16km (10 miles)*

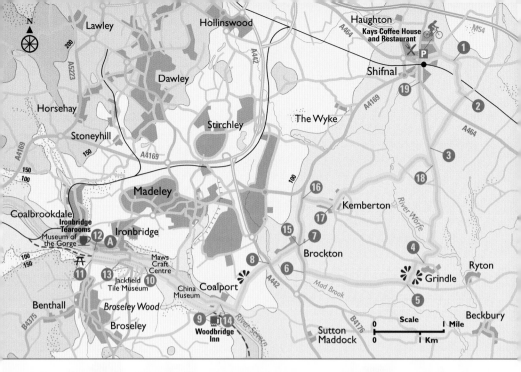

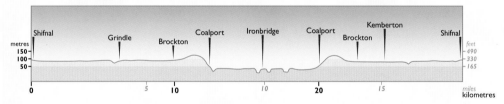

11 TL and immediately TR to visit Benthall Edge picnic site.

To continue route, TR and cross iron bridge into Ironbridge.

12 Various museums are SP at end of bridge. After visit, re-cross bridge. At end of bridge, TL at TJ onto road.

13 TL at TJ, SP Ironbridge B4373. Cross river and TR, SP Coalport, onto a narrow road with a 15 MPH speed limit.

14 TL at TJ, no SP, and rejoin inward route for steep climb out of Severn Gorge. SO at XR, over A442, SP Brockton.

15 TL at TJ, SP Shifnal. Continue and immediately before junction with A4169:

16 TR, SP Kemberton.

17 TL at TJ, SP Shifnal.

25km (15.5 miles)

18 TL at TJ into Hinnington Road, no SP. Continue on this road into Shifnal.

19 TL in Shifnal, SP Sherrifhales. Pass under railway bridge and TR. Immediately TR into Aston Road and retrace route back to car park and railway station to complete the ride.

30km (18.5 miles)

Places of interest along the route

A Ironbridge

The World Heritage site at Ironbridge Gorge marks the building of the world's first cast iron bridge, constructed to span the River Severn. This advance in technology was an important part of the Industrial Revolution and today nine different museums describe the site and its history, including a Museum of Iron, Jackfield Tile Museum, Coalport China Museum, Blists Hill Victorian Town and Maws Craft Centre. Cafés and tearooms. The main seasonal opening is between Easter and November, daily 100–1700; during the winter some smaller sites close. Telephone Ironbridge Tourist Information Centre for more details on (01952) 432166 or visit www.ironbridge.org

Food and drink

Kays Coffee House and Restaurant, Shifnal
Serves snacks and meals.

Woodbridge Inn, Coalport
Bar meals available.

Ironbridge Tearooms, Ironbridge
Teas and light meals.

The Iron Bridge

HATTON AND PACKWOOD

Route information

Distance   29.5km (18.5 miles)

Grade   Moderate

Terrain   Tarmac road throughout. There are a few inclines but nothing too challenging. A section of B and a short section of A road can be busy.

Time to allow   2–3 hours.

Getting there by car   Hatton Station, the start of the route, is just off the A4177/B4439, a short distance from Hatton village and approximately 6km (4 miles) north west of Warwick.

Getting there by train   There is a regular service to Hatton Station. For travel information telephone (08457) 484950 or visit www.nationalrail.co.uk

Starting from Hatton Station, the route heads north through Little Shrewley and continues along attractive quiet lanes to Rowington Green. A stretch of the B4439 takes you across two canals – the Grand Union Canal and the Stratford-upon-Avon Canal – in quick succession. Turning north the route leads past the attractive Packwood House and then Baddesley Clinton (both in the care of the National Trust). Turning south again, past Hay Wood and Hatton Country World, where a final refreshment stop can be taken before finishing the ride at the station.

Places of interest along the route

A **Packwood House, Packwood**

Looking older than it is, Packwood House was built in the twentieth century evoking the memory of Tudor times. It was created by Graham Baron Ash and the interiors reflect the period of 1918–1939. The house is surrounded by yew hedges clipped into large solid shapes, which are well appreciated from the roadside. Kiosk serves light refreshments. Open April–October, Wednesday–Sunday 1330–1630. Charge. Telephone (01564) 783294; www.ntrustsevern.org.uk

B **Baddesley Clinton**

The moated manor house at Baddesley Clinton has interiors that reflect the Elizabethan era. The house was a haven for persecuted Catholics and has three priest holes where they could hide. The house has changed little and is surrounded by gardens and walks. Also thatched summerhouse. Restaurant. Open March to October, Wednesday–Sunday 1330–1700. Charge. Telephone (01684) 855364; www.ntrustsevern.org.uk

C **Hatton Country World**

You will need plenty of time if you chose to visit Hatton Country World, as there are a wide variety of activities. Based around a farm park, home to all the usual animals, there is factory shopping, an antiques centre, nature trails and several tearooms. Also sheep dog displays, tractor rides and a children's entertainer. Café (free admission). Open all year, daily 1000–1700. Charge for admission to farm park. Telephone (01926) 84341; www.hattonworld.com

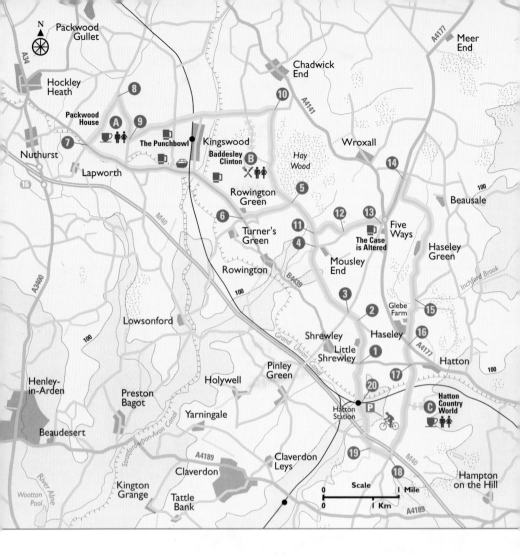

N

Packwood
Gullet

Hockley
Heath

Packwood
House

A

Nuthurst

7

8

9

The Punchbowl

Lapworth

Kingswood

Baddesley
Clinton **B**

Rowington
Green

6

Turner's
Green

Rowington

10

Chadwick
End

A4141

Hay
Wood

5

11

4

B4439

Wroxall

12

13

The Case
is Altered

Mousley
End

Meer
End

Beausale

Five
Ways

Haseley
Green

Inchford Brook

14

3

Lowsonford

Henley-
in-Arden

Preston
Bagot

Holywell

Yarningale

Beaudesert

Pinley
Green

Claverdon

Claverdon
Leys

Kington
Grange

Tattle
Bank

A4189

Shrewley

Little
Shrewley

2

Glebe
Farm

Haseley

15

16

1

17

20

Hatton
Station

P

Hatton

A4177

Hatton
Country
World **C**

19

M40

18

Hampton
on the Hill

A4189

Scale

0 ————————— 1 Mile

0 ————————— 1 Km

Grand Union Canal

Stratford-upon-Avon Canal

River Alne

Wootton
Pool

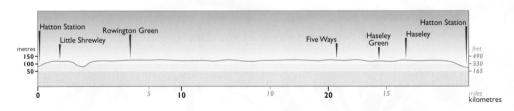

	metres	feet
	150	490
	100	330
	50	165

Hatton Station

Little Shrewley

Rowington Green

Five Ways

Haseley
Green

Haseley

Hatton Station

0   5   10   10   20   15   miles
kilometres

Route description

From station car park, exit to road and TR at TJ, no SP. Cross Grand Union Canal.

1 SO at XR, SP Little Shrewley. Continue along Mill Lane.

2 TL at TJ, SP Mousley End/Warwick.

3 SO at XR, SP Mousley End. Cycle downhill along tree-lined lane.

4 TL, SP Rowington/Chadwick End.

5 TL, SP Rowington/Lapworth.

6 TR at XR onto B4439, SP Lapworth/Hockley Heath (6.5km/4 miles). Pass store and pubs.

7 TR at XR into Grove Lane, SP Knowle.

8 TR at TJ, no SP but opposite Packwood House SP (11km/7 miles). Pass Packwood House on RHS.

9 TL at TJ, SP Baddesley Clinton/Chadwick End. Pass entrance to Baddesley Clinton on RHS.

10 TR, SP Mousley End/Hay Wood. Pass Hay Wood on LHS.

11 TL, no SP but gateway opposite junction. Gentle climb ahead.

18.5km (11.5 miles)

12 TL at TJ into Case Lane, SP Haseley Knob/Balsall Common.

13 TL at TJ, no SP. SO at roundabout along A4177, SP Haseley Knob/Balsall Common/Stonebridge.

14 TR, SP Haseley Knob/Beausale. Immediately TR, SP Haseley Green.

15 TR at TJ, no SP (24km/15 miles). Pass Glebe Farm on RHS and enter Haseley.

16 SO at XR, SP Hatton Green/Norton Lindsey.

17 SO at XR, SP Hatton Country World/Norton Lindsey. Pass Hatton Country World on LHS.

18 TR, SP Hatton Station/Pinley.

19 TR, SP Hatton Station.

20 TR, no SP, and return to station to finish the ride. *29.5km (18.5 miles)*

Food and drink

There is a convenience store and two pubs near Lapworth. Refreshments are also available at Packwood House, Baddesley Clinton and Hatton Country World. The Case is Altered, near Five Ways, sells real ale but does not provide meals.

The Punchbowl, near Lapworth
Bar meals available.

HINCKLEY TO BOSWORTH FIELDS

Route information

Distance 31.5km (19.5 miles)

Grade Easy

Terrain Quiet lanes and canal towpath, some sections of which can be overgrown in places.

Time to allow 2–4 hours.

Getting there by car Hinckley is 19km (12 miles) south west of Leicester on the A447, close to the A5 and M69 north of Coventry. The railway station, the start of the route, is close to the A447 which passes though the town centre. There are several car parks in the town.

Getting there by train Hinckley is served by trains running between Birmingham and Nottingham via Nuneaton. For travel information telephone (08457) 484950 or visit www.nationalrail.co.uk

From the market town of Hinckley the route skirts round the MIRA road vehicle test site with secret testing facilities for car manufacturers. Quiet lanes lead to Bosworth Battlefield, where a visitor centre tells the history of the Wars of the Roses. The route passes close to the spot where King Richard III was killed. After leaving the visitor centre, the route takes to the towpath of the Ashby Canal to make a winding return to Hinckley.

Route description

Start from Hinckley Station, heading north, to SO at XR into Station Street, SP Town Centre.

1 TL into Lancaster Road, SP Bus Station/Library. TR at XR (traffic lights) into Regents Street, SP Town Centre/Earl Shilton.

2 TL at traffic lights (opposite Union Inn, road SP No Motor Vehicles) and then TR into Lower Bond Street (at Duke of Rutland pub). Pass Hinckley and District Museum on LHS and TL at traffic lights (opposite police station), SP Wykin/Stoke Golding.

3 TL into Wykin Road (main road bears R with a convenience store straight ahead). Pass Redmoor High School on RHS.

4 SO at roundabout, SP Wykin. Continue through Wykin and cross Ashby Canal.

5 TR at XR into Stoke Lane, SP Stoke Golding/Dadlington.

6 TL at XR, SP Upton/Fenny Drayton.

7 TL at TJ, SP Upton/Fenny Drayton/Atherstone. Shortly afterwards TR, SP Upton. Continue into Upton.

8 TR in Upton (effectively SO), SP Shenton/Market Bosworth.

9 TR at TJ, SP Dadlington/Market Bosworth. Go round corner then TL, SP Sutton Cheney. Continue into Shenton.

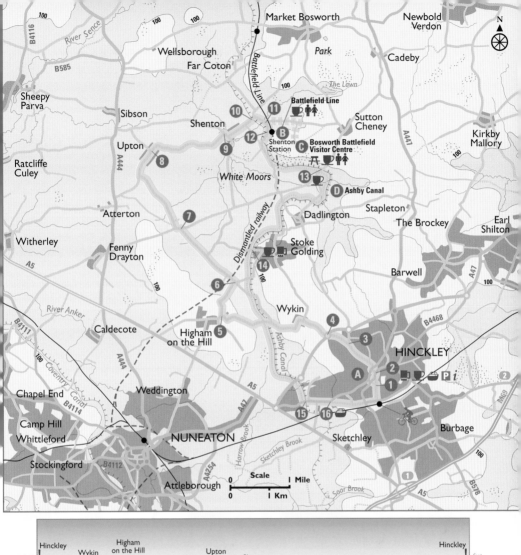

10 Pass under canal bridge and TR at TJ, SP Sutton Cheney/Dadlington.

11 To visit Bosworth Battlefield, TL under railway bridge, SP Sutton Cheney/Cadeby. Continue and TR, SP Bosworth Battlefield Visitor Centre. After visit, retrace route passing under railway and TL at TJ, SP Dadlington.

16km (10 miles)

Otherwise, SO to continue route.

12 Pass entrance to Battlefield Line on LHS. Cross canal bridge and TL to descend to towpath, SP Stoke Golding.

13 Near Bridge 34 at Sutton Cheney, on opposite bank (accessed by road bridge) there is a tearoom and boat trips.

14 To visit Stock Golding, leave canal at Bridge 25 and TR over canal bridge (25.5km/ 16 miles).

Otherwise, continue towards Hinckley until shortly after Trinity Canal Basin and leave canal towpath **before** passing under A47.

15 TL onto A47.

16 TR into Strathmore Road (just before shops). TR at TJ into Westfield Road (effectively SO). SO at roundabout, SP Station. TR into station car park to finish the ride.

31.5km (19.5 miles)

Places of interest along the route

Ⓐ Hinckley
In 1640, Hinckley was the first hosiery manufacturing town in Leicestershire to install a stocking machine. **Hinckley and District Museum**, Lower Bond Street, is housed in a row of restored 17th-century thatched cottages, once used for framework knitting. The museum describes the town's history from prehistoric times to the Middle Ages, and has displays on the hosiery, boot and shoe making industries. Tearoom and cottage garden. Open Easter Monday to October, Saturday and Bank Holiday Mondays 1000–1600, Sunday 1400–1700. Small charge. Contact the Tourist Information Centre for more information on (01455) 635106.

Ⓑ Battlefield Line, Shenton Station
A preserved steam railway which offers a 16km (10 mile) round trip between Shenton and Shackerstone. Tea room, museum and display of rolling stock at Shackerstone station. Pottery shop at Shenton. Museum open March to October, weekends only 1130–1730. Trains run March to October, each Sunday. There are additional steam and diesel train journeys May to September, each Saturday; diesel only July and August, each Wednesday. Charge. Telephone (01827) 880754.

Ⓒ Bosworth Battlefield Visitor Centre, Sutton Cheney
The historic site of the Battle of Bosworth, fought in 1485 when King Richard III was defeated by the future Henry VII. A visitor centre contains a film theatre, book and gift shop, information point and café. Also country park with picnic areas and battle trails. Special medieval events throughout the year. Visitor centre open April to October, Monday–Saturday 1100–1700, Sunday and Bank Holidays 1100–1800. Charge for exhibition but other facilities free. Telephone (01455) 290429.

Ⓓ Ashby Canal
The Ashby Canal was originally intended to be a through route from the River Trent at Burton to the Coventry Canal near Bedworth. This plan was repeatedly shelved but in 1792 the Ashby Canal Company was formed to build a canal to service the local coalfields. The last load of coal was carried along the canal in 1970. Today visitors can take a 40-minute narrowboat trip from Sutton Cheney Wharf. Refreshments available. Trips operate Easter to September, weekends; July and August, daily. Charge. Telephone (01455) 213838 for more information.

Food and drink

Plenty of choice in Hinckley, as would be expected from a market town. Refreshments are available at the Bosworth Battlefield Visitor Centre. Stoke Golding has a couple of pubs that serve bar meals and there are several teashops along the towpath of the Ashby Canal.

TAMWORTH AND TWYCROSS

Route information

- **Distance** 33.5km (21 miles)

- **Grade** Easy

- **Terrain** Generally flat with a few short hills. A short section of canal towpath is used.

- **Time to allow** 2–4 hours. Allow extra time to visit Twycross Zoo.

- **Getting there by car** Tamworth is 22.5km (14 miles) north east of Birmingham on the A51, A5 and A453, close to the M42, junction 10. There are several car parks in the town centre. The route starts from the railway station.

- **Getting there by train** Tamworth is served by trains from Birmingham, London and Derby. For travel information telephone (08457) 484950 or visit www.nationalrail.co.uk

A gentle ride through rich arable countryside. The route climbs out of Tamworth in two stages – the first climb out of the Tame Valley is followed by a flat interlude and the second, steeper but shorter climb takes the cyclist up to Twycross Zoo. The zoo is probably most famous for its training of the chimpanzees used in the PG Tips advertisements. The return to Tamworth passes through Polesworth with its abbey and old buildings. To avoid the traffic which has become inevitable so close to a large town, the route out of and into Tamworth follows a section of the towpath along the Coventry Canal.

Places of interest along the route

A Tamworth Castle, Tamworth

A classic Norman motte and bailey castle, built from sandstone. It is thought to date from the 1180s. The castle has changed hands many times over the years until being bought by Tamworth Corporation and opened to the public in 1899. The castle is signposted from the town centre and would make a good place to visit at the end of the ride. Charge. Telephone (01827) 709629; www.tamworthcastle.freeserve. co.uk

B Twycross Zoo, near Twycross

Twycross Zoo specialises in monkeys and apes but is home to the full range of zoo animals and has a successful breeding program, ensuring lots of interest in the babies. Pets corner and adventure playground with extra summer attractions including donkey rides and miniature train rides. Café. Open all year, daily (except Christmas day) 1000–1700 (1600 in winter). Charge. Telephone (01827) 880250; www.twycrosszoo.com

C Polesworth

The Benedictine abbey at Polesworth dates back to the 9th century. The first Abbess was St Editha, thought to be the elder sister of King Alfred the Great. The parish church of St Editha was converted from the abbey church and the nave was originally built in the 12th century. Free admission at all reasonable times.

Route description

Start outside Tamworth Station and set off south towards the roundabout, where TL along cycle path on LHS of Saxon Drive.

1 On approach to next roundabout, TL across front of a petrol station and go over bridge. At roundabout, follow cycle path along LHS turn, SP Bolehall/Amington/Shuttington.

2 As cycle path ends, TL into Amington Road for climb and descent.

3 TL at foot of hill into June Crescent. Immediately TR onto path that leads to Coventry Canal, no SP. TL along canal towpath. Continue, to pass under bridge 65.

4 Immediately after passing under bridge 65, TL to leave canal. TL onto road over bridge.

5 TL at TJ, no SP. Follow road towards Austrey.

6 TL at TJ, SP Appleby Magna/Orton-on-the-Hill. **11km (7 miles)**

7 TR onto main road, SP Orton-on-the-Hill. Follow road towards Orton-on-the-Hill for short, steep climb.

8 At top of climb, to visit Twycross Zoo, TL at XR into Norton Lane, SP Little Orton/Norton.

a TR at TJ onto A444 with CARE, SP Nuneaton/Twycross/Sibson, and continue to zoo. **16.5km (10.5 miles)**

Otherwise, to follow main route, TR at XR, SP Warton/Polesworth.

9 TR at TJ (triangular), SP Warton/Polesworth.

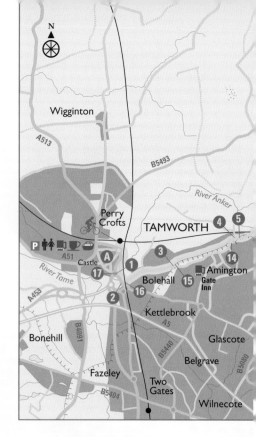

10 SO at XR, SP Polesworth. As you descend into Polesworth, the entrance to abbey grounds is on LHS through medieval gateway (about 200m before TJ).

11 TR at TJ into Station Road, SP Shuttington (village centre is on LHS).

12 TL at TJ (effectively SO), SP Shuttington/Amington/Tamworth.

13 TL at TJ, SP Amington/Tamworth.

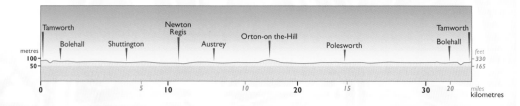

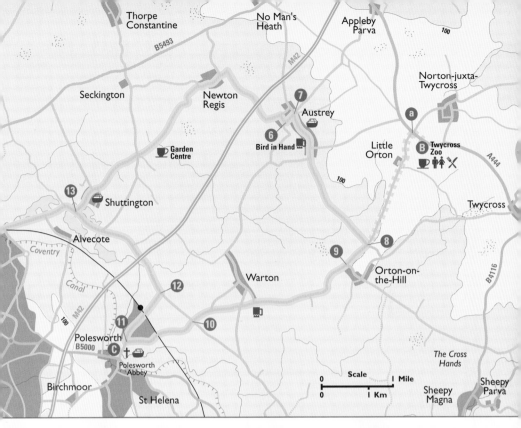

14 TR at roundabout, SP Amington. Cross canal bridge and drop down to towpath. TR along towpath (**not** back under bridge).

15 Leave canal at bridge 71 and TR onto main road (**not** along June Crescent).

16 On approach to roundabout system at foot of hill, TR onto cycle path, no SP. LHF immediately before going under railway viaduct, and follow path up to roundabout and to RHS over river bridge.

17 TR at roundabout, along cycle path (Saxon Drive). Follow cycle path to the next roundabout where TR to finish the ride at the station. *33.5km (21 miles)*

Food and drink

There is plenty of choice in Tamworth and convenience stores in Shuttington, Austrey, and Polesworth. Most villages passed along the way have a pub. Newton Regis Garden Centre (after Shuttington) has a café and refreshments are available at Twycross Zoo.

 Bird in Hand, Austrey
Bar meals available.

Gate Inn, Tamworth
On the Coventry Canal by Bridge 69. Real ale and meals.

Route information

 Distance   34.5km (21.5 miles)

Grade   Strenuous

 Terrain   The majority of the route follows quiet lanes, but there are several hills including a steep climb out of the Churnet valley.

 Time to allow   2–4 hours.

Getting there by car   Cheadle is 12.5km (8 miles) east of Stoke-on-Trent, on the A521 and A522. There are a number of car parks in the town, close to the A522.

Getting there by train   The nearest railway station is in Uttoxeter. For travel information telephone (08457) 484950 or visit www.nationalrail.co.uk

A route through the Staffordshire countryside. In order to avoid using busier roads, this otherwise circular route leaves and returns to Cheadle by the same road, giving cyclists the opportunity of a swooping descent from Freehay at the end of the ride. The first two thirds of the route take generally gentle climbs and descents to pass Croxden Abbey and reach Alton. Here the terrain changes to a steeply sloping wooded valley with the River Churnet running along the foot. The optional extension

to Oakamoor gives cyclists a last chance for refreshments before the steep (between 1:7 and 1:5) climb out of the valley, up Stoney Dale and then down to the Highwayman pub. Listen for screams and the rumble of roller-coasters near Alton, as you are within earshot of Alton Towers leisure park.

Places of interest along the route

Ⓐ Cheadle
The old market town of Cheadle has a variety of architectural styles. The magnificent catholic church was designed by Pugin and its 61m (200 foot) high spire dominates the town. On a more modest scale, there is a Georgian market square and a Tudor frontage in the High Street. The Buttery Cross dates as far back as 1652. For more information on local amenities, contact Stoke-on-Trent Tourist Information Centre on (01782) 236000.

Ⓑ Croxden Abbey, Croxden
The abbey at Croxden was established by Bertramn de Verdon in 1176 for the Cistercian order. Unfortunately, at some point the current road has been driven across the site, splitting the main church in two. The most imposing remains are those of the west wall with its magnificent gothic arch. Free access at all reasonable times.

Alton Towers

Route description

To start from Uttoxeter railway station, leave Uttoxeter on A522 then B5030, heading towards Ashbourne. Join the route at direction 10 where SO to stay on B5030, SP Ashbourne.

To start from Cheadle, cycle through the town on the A522 heading towards Uttoxeter.

1 TL into Mill Road, no SP. Descend gently out of town and then climb steeply through a hairpin bend towards Freehay.

2 TL at XR, SP Alton. Immediately TR at roundabout, SP Great Gate. Descend, gently at first then steeply after a camping site on RHS.

3 TR at TJ at foot of steep descent, no SP.
5km (3 miles)

4 LHF, SP Croxden/Alton. Cross ford with care (a foot bridge is available at side of ford).

5 TR into Croxden Lane, SP Croxden Abbey. Continue along Croxden Lane past abbey.
8km (5 miles)

6 TR at TJ, SP Hollington/Tean.

7 TL into narrow lane, SP Stramshall.

8 LHF, no SP, (RHF named Watery Lane). Continue towards Stramshall.
12km (7.5 miles)

9 TL at TJ into St Michaels Road.

10 To return to Uttoxeter station, TR.

Otherwise, to continue route, TL at TJ onto B5030, SP Ashbourne.

11 SO at roundabout, SP Rocester/ Ashbourne. Take CARE on this busy road. Continue for 1km (0.6 mile) to:

12 TL, SP Crakemarsh.

13 TL, no SP (18.5km/11.5 miles). Climb gently away from junction and after 1km (0.6 mile), cross ford with CARE (no footbridge this time!)

14 TL at TJ and immediately TR into Nabb Lane.

15 TL at TJ onto B5032. Immediately TR into Uttoxeter Road, SP Alton/Farley. Descend steeply through village of Alton.

16 Before crossing bridge over River Churnet, TL at wall mounted post box, no SP. Pass Alton Bridge Hotel on LHS after junction.

17 TR, no SP, into Horse Road (24.5km/ 15 miles). Continue along Churnet valley, passing café on LHS.

18 To visit Oakamoor for refreshments, TR at TJ.

Otherwise, to continue main route, TL at TJ, no SP but youth hostel SP mounted on telegraph pole here (27km/17 miles). Climb steeply out of Churnet valley and after a short decent:

19 TR at XR onto B5032 near Highwayman pub, no SP.
29.5km (18.5 miles)

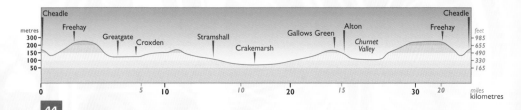

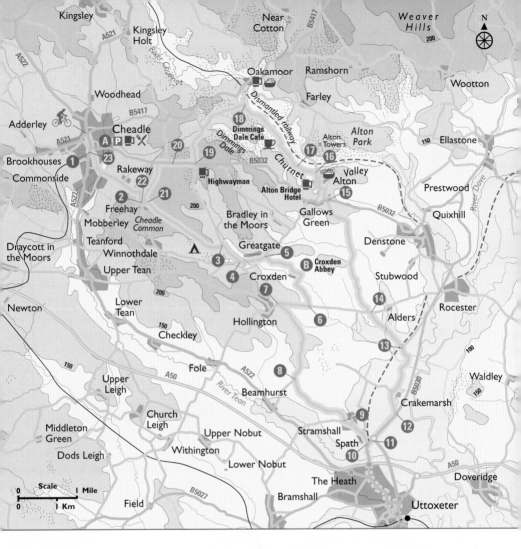

20 TL, SP Freehay/Mobberley.

21 TR at roundabout, SP Cheadle/Freehay/
Wirrothdale.

22 TR at XR, SP Cheadle. Descend carefully
around hairpin bends and climb gently back
into Cheadle.

23 TR at TJ onto A522, no SP, and return to
Cheadle town centre to finish the ride.

34.5km (21.5 miles)

Food and drink

*There are several pubs and restaurants
in Cheadle and a variety of pubs and
shops in Alton and Oakamoor.*

Alton Bridge Hotel, Alton
*In a pleasant setting, just outside Alton
at direction 16.*

Dimmings Dale Café, near Alton
Passed en route.

NANTWICH AND WRENBURY

Route information

 Distance 36km (22.5 miles)

Grade Easy

Terrain Mostly flat, quiet lanes. There is a gradual climb after Cholmondeley Castle, bypassed by the short cut.

Time to allow 3–4 hours.

Getting there by car Acton is 2km (1 mile) west of Nantwich on the A534. The ride starts from the free car park, opposite The Star pub.

Getting there by train The nearest railway station is at Nantwich. For travel information telephone (08457) 484950 or visit www.nationalrail.co.uk

A route along quiet, scenic lanes. From the attractive market town of Nantwich the route heads west past Cholmondeley Castle and then loops around to head east, through Wrenbury and back to Nantwich. Some sections of the route run alongside the Shropshire Union and the Llangollen Canals. The route can be shortened to 22.5km (14 miles), bypassing Cholmondeley Castle and avoiding the gradual climb.

Places of interest along the route

A Nantwich

A prosperous market town since Roman times, on the River Weaver and the Shropshire Union Canal. The town was the centre of the salt mining industry. Today the town's market is held each Tuesday morning and all day Thursday and Saturday. The sandstone **Church of St Mary**, Church Lane, is the focal point of the town centre. It was originally constructed during the 14th century and much restored during the 19th century. Open all year, by donation. Telephone (01270) 820534 for more information **Nantwich Museum**, Pillory Street, gives an insight into the life and times of the town. Roman and medieval treasures, and a cheese-making display. Open 1030–1630, summer Monday–Saturday; winter Tuesday–Saturday. Free admission. Telephone (01270) 627104. **Dorfold Hall** is a Jacobean house built in 1616. The panelled rooms contain fine furnishings and portraits. Open April to October, Tuesday and Bank Holiday Mondays 1400–1700. Charge. Telephone (01270) 625245. An attractive iron aqueduct takes the Shropshire Union Canal across the main road and just to the north west of the town is Nantwich Basin. This was once the terminus of the Chester Canal, which ran between Nantwich and Ellesmere Port, and the old canalside cheese warehouses are still standing. There is a boatyard here, selling maps,

Cholmondeley Castle

books, gifts and groceries amongst the chandlery items. Also café. Open daily, telephone (01270) 625122 to confirm times.

Ⓑ Cholmondeley Castle Garden, near Nantwich

Ornamental gardens and rare farm animals, tearoom and lakeside picnic area. Open April to September, Wednesday, Thursday, Sunday and Bank Holiday Monday 1130–1700. Charge. Telephone (01829) 720383.

Ⓒ Wrenbury

A attractive village approximately 0.5km (0.3 mile) from the Llangollen Canal. At Wrenbury Wharf is a restored warehouse and a former mill, centred on a lift bridge over the canal.

Food and drink

Plenty of pubs and cafés in Nantwich and a café at Nantwich Basin.

🍺 **The Star, Acton**
Bar meals served at lunch times. Outside seating.

🍺 **Dusty Miller, Wrenbury Wharf**
In a former 19th-century mill. Meals available. Canalside garden.

Route description

To start from Nantwich station, follow SP Town Centre. TL at roundabout into Waterlode. Continue to traffic lights where TL onto A534, SP Chester. Continue into Acton.

To start from Acton, TR out of car park (opposite The Star) and immediately TL by Acton church.

1 Take first TL into Swanley Lane. SO at three-way junction, SP Wrenbury. Cross canal, SP Larden Green/Chorley. Follow road through these villages to TJ.

2 To take short cut, TL, SP Wrenbury, and pick up route at direction 10, where TL, SP Nantwich.

To follow main route, TR at TJ, SP Cholmondeley.   ***9km (5.5 miles)***

3 SO at XR into Cholmondeley village.

4 To visit Cholmondley Castle, TR at castle entrance.

Otherwise, stay on this road, with views of castle and lake on RHS.

5 TL opposite second castle entrance, no SP, for gentle climb to Hampton Post (excellent views of Cheshire on RHS).

6 TL at XR, SP Hampton Green.

7 TL at TJ onto A41. Immediately TL, SP Bickley/Marbury.   ***16.5km (10.5 miles)***

8 SO at XR over A49, SP Wrenbury.

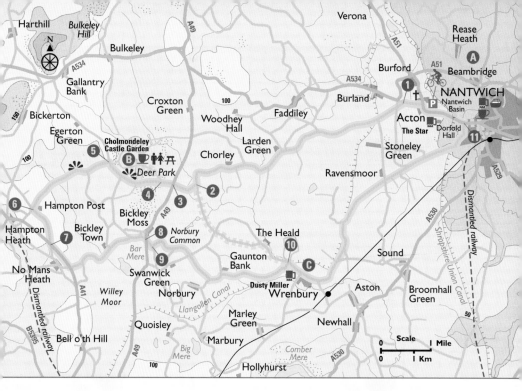

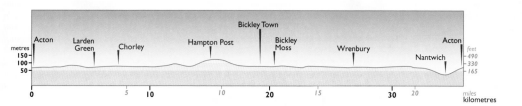

9 Take first TL, no SP. Keep L SP Wrenbury. Pass Barn Books (antiquarian and second hand bookshop). Continue into Wrenbury, joining the canal.

---

10 TR at TJ, no SP (25.5km/16 miles). Cross canal via lift bridge (pub on RHS). Follow this road through Wrenbury, SP Nantwich. Cross canal three times and enter Nantwich.

33.5km (21 miles)

11 TR at TJ to visit Nantwich or to return to Nantwich Station.

Otherwise, TL at TJ, SP Wrenbury. Continue under canal. Pass Nantwich Basin on RHS and finish the ride in Acton, opposite The Star pub.

36km (22.5 miles)

WELLINGTON, LONGDON UPON TERN AND HIGH ERCALL

Route information

 Distance 43km (27 miles)

 Grade Easy

 Terrain Quiet lanes and B roads.

 Time to allow 2–3 hours.

 Getting there by car Wellington is 16km (10 miles) east of Shrewsbury, close to the M54, junction 7, and the A5 and A442. Park in the free car park at the leisure and civic centre in the centre of town.

 Getting there by train There is a railway station at Wellington. For travel information telephone (08457) 484950 or visit www.nationalrail.co.uk

The attractions on this route are the Shropshire scenery and panoramic views. The route passes through mainly arable farmland and skylarks are often heard here above the corn fields.

Places of interest along the route

Ⓐ Rivers Roden and Tern

The route passes the confluence of these two rivers, and the meeting point and weir is worth a visit. The River Roden rises near Northwood, flows south east through Wem and then south into the River Tern. The River Tern rises near Madeley, flows south west through Market Drayton and then south into the River Severn between Atcham and Wroxeter.

Route description

TR out of Wellington leisure centre car park into Victoria Road. SO at mini roundabout. Then SO at traffic lights SP Admaston.

1 SO at roundabout, SP Admaston.

2 Keep SO, SP Wrockwardine, and gradually climb for good views.

3 TR in Wrockwardine, SP Admaston. TL by church, SP Allscott. Descend, enjoying the views.

4 TL at TJ onto B4394, no SP. Pass under railway bridge and TR, no SP.

5 TR at TJ, SP Longdon upon Tern. Continue on this road.

Wellington

6 TL at TJ, SP Longdon (8km/5 miles). Cross River Tern.

7 Take first TL, no SP.

8 SO, SP Withington.

9 Continue through Isombridge. Expansive views across to the Welsh hills and the Wrekin.

10 Cross River Roden. To visit confluence of Rivers Roden and Tern, TL at XR for 1km (0.6 mile).

Otherwise, to continue main route, SO at XR, SP Withington. Continue through Withington, gradually climbing.

11 TR, no SP but SP 7.5T for Access. Good views on LHS.

12 SO at XR, SP Haughmond Hill (15km/ 9.5 miles). Gradually climb.

13 TR at XR, SP Astley. Panoramic views on LHS.

14 TR at TJ, SP Newport B5062. Pass Roden Nursery (café) on RHS.

15 TL, SP Poynton. Continue into Poynton Green.

16 TR in Poynton Green, SP High Ercall.
                    23km (14.5 miles)

17 TR at TJ, SP High Ercall. Continue through High Ercall, passing Cleveland Arms pub on LHS.

18 SO, SP Telford. TL at mini roundabout, SP Crudington.

19 SO at XR (over A442), SP Newport B5062.

20 TR, SP Kynnersley.   *31.5km (19.5 miles)*

21 SO at TJ, SP Kynnersley, and continue through Kynnersley (Spitfire aircraft propeller and model Spitfire in garden on RHS).

22 Keep R, SP Preston, and continue through Preston.

23 TR at XR, SP Horton.

24 Take third exit at Leegomery roundabout, SP Leegomery (40km/25 miles). TR at mini roundabout, SP Wellington.

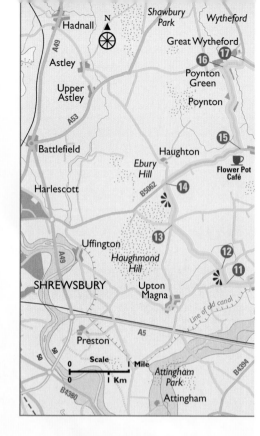

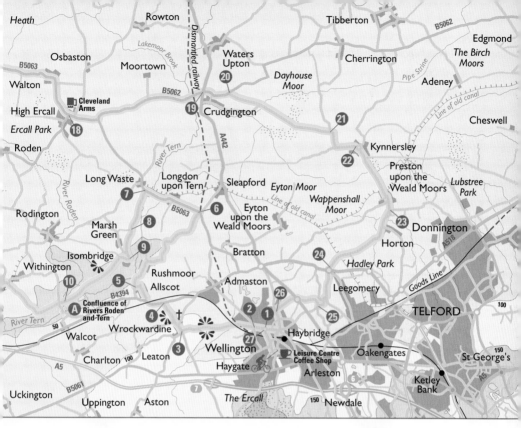

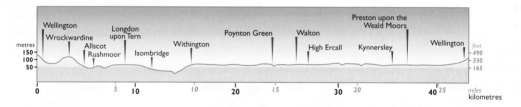

25 TR at mini roundabout, SP Wellington.
SO at Apley roundabout, SP Wellington.

26 TL at roundabout, SP Town Centre. Then
TR, SP Station.

27 TL at roundabout, SP Wellington
Centre. Rejoin outward route. Continue SO
and return to car park to finish the ride.

43km (27 miles)

Food and drink

*There is a café at Wellington leisure
centre, the start of the route.*

Flower Pot Café, Roden
Situation within Roden Nursery.

Cleveland Arms, High Ercall
Approximately half way around the route.

BRETFORTON AND STRATFORD-UPON-AVON

Route information

Distance 49.5km (31miles)

Grade Easy

Terrain Most of the route is over tarmac. A section of cycleway (converted railway track) is used which has a generally excellent surface and only deteriorates in the last mile.

Time to allow 3–6 hours.

Getting there by car Bretforton is 6km (4 miles) east of Evesham on the B4035. As you turn into the village there is a small car park by the church.

Getting there by train The nearest railway station is at Honeybourne, passed en route. For travel information telephone (08457) 484950 or visit www.nationalrail.co.uk

Starting from the attractive village of Bretforton, the route heads north east along flat or gently undulating roads. At Long Marston the track bed of the old Honeybourne railway is joined and this provides 8km (5 miles) of pleasant flat cycling to the outskirts of Stratford-upon-Avon. A route through the centre of town takes you past most of the places of interest before the route heads west again to Ann Hathaway's cottage. The last part of the ride is through the valley of the River Avon, passing several villages and pubs.

Places of interest along the route

A Domestic Fowl Trust, Honeybourne

The trust incorporates Honeybourne Rare Breeds and works in the conservation of rare and traditional farm animals and poultry. Children's play area. Light refreshments and ice cream for sale. Open all year, daily 1030–1700. Telephone (01386) 833083.

B Stratford-upon-Avon

Famed as the birthplace of William Shakespeare, tourism has been established in the town for a long time – the first big celebrations in Shakespeare's honour were organised in 1789. For information on the town's attractions, see Route 1.

C Anne Hathaway's Cottage, Shottery

Home to descendants of the Hathaway family until the 19th century, Anne Hathaway's Cottage is situated in Shottery, just outside Stratford. The thatched farmhouse contains original furniture and there is a traditional cottage garden. Opening times are as for Shakespeare's birthplace (see Route 1). Charge.

D Middle Littleton Tithe Barn, Middle Littleton

Built in the 13th century, Middle Littleton Tithe Barn is still in use as a farm building. Tithe barns were used by the local community to store produce over winter, and this one built of blue lias stone is one of many countrywide managed by the National Trust. Open April to October, daily 1400-1700. Small charge.

Food and drink

There are lots of places for refreshment along the route. Stratford-upon-Avon has lots of choice and there are pubs in Bretforton, Honeybourne, Shottery, Welford-on-Avon, Barton, Cleve Prior and North Littleton. Bretforton and Honeybourne also have convenience stores.

Route description

If starting from Honeybourne railway station, leave station and TL. Continue to direction 6.

If starting from Bretforton, leave car park and head along Bridge Street, passing steps to church on RHS. Cross a small bridge to:

1 TL at TJ, no SP. Cycle along lane with fields on RHS. Pass farm on RHS (on 90 degree right-handed bend).

2 TL at TJ opposite two tracks, no SP (RHS track has cattle grid).

3 SO at XR, SP Honeybourne (seat on LHS at junction). Enter Honeybourne.

4 TR at TJ opposite Green Close, no SP.

5 TL at XR, SP Bickmarsh/Bidford-on-Avon. Pass Domestic Fowl Trust on LHS, then Honeybourne railway station.

6 TR at XR, SP Pebworth/Broad Marston/Mickleton (7km/4.5 miles). Continue through Pebworth.

7 TR at TJ, SP Long Marston/Welford.

8 TL at TJ, SP Welford (seat on LHS).

9 TR opposite telephone box into Wyre Lane, no SP.

10 TL onto cycleway at Wyre Lane crossing (13.5km/8.5 miles). Follow this well graded cycleway, crossing one road. At end of track:

11 Take tarmac path on LHS. When road is reached, TR along cycleway, following it to L at large roundabout. Follow cycleway to next roundabout and TR, SP Town Centre (cycleway continues SO). After 150m, TR, SP Town Centre only. Pass Civic Hall LHS.

12 TR at XR, no SP (clock RHS, SP No Entry SO). Pass Swan Hotel on LHS. As road bears hard left, dismount to cross road and continue along Waterside, passing first canal boat basin and then Royal Shakespeare Company on LHS.

River Avon, Stratford-upon-Avon

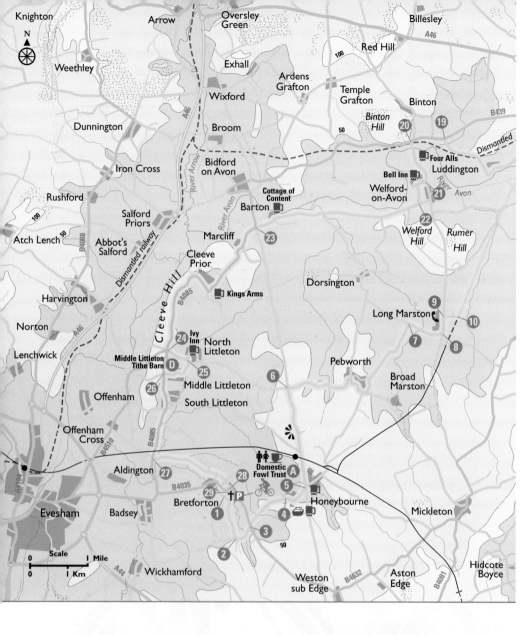

Knighton

Arrow

Oversley
Green

Billesley

A46

N

Weethley

Red Hill

100

Exhall

Ardens
Grafton

Temple
Grafton

Binton

Dunnington

Wixford

Binton
Hill

Binton

20

19

B439

Broom

50

Four Alls

Luddington

Dismantled

Iron Cross

River Arrow

Bidford
on Avon

Bell Inn

Welford-
on-Avon

21

River Avon

Cottage of
Content

River Avon

Rushford

Salford
Priors

Barton

22

100

Abbot's
Salford

Marcliff

23

Welford
Hill

Rumer
Hill

Atch Lench

50

B4088

Cleeve
Prior

Dorsington

Harvington

Dismantled railway

Cleeve Hill

B4085

Kings Arms

Long Marston

9

10

Norton

A46

Ivy
Inn

24

North
Littleton

7

8

Lenchwick

Pebworth

Middle Littleton
Tithe Barn

D

25

Broad
Marston

Offenham

26

Middle Littleton

South Littleton

Offenham
Cross

B4510

B4085

Aldington

27

Domestic
Fowl Trust

A

B4035

5

Honeybourne

Mickleton

A4184

28

Evesham

29

Bretforton

P

1

4

3

Badsey

50

2

Scale

1 Mile

0   1 Km

A44

Wickhamford

Weston
sub Edge

B4632

Aston
Edge

B4081

Hidcote
Boyce

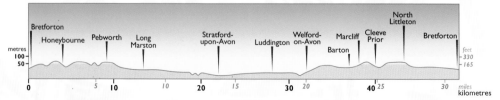

metres
100
50

Bretforton

Honeybourne

Pebworth

Long
Marston

Stratford-
upon-Avon

Luddington

Welford-
on-Avon

Marcliff

Cleeve
Prior

North
Littleton

Bretforton

feet
330
165

0   5   10   10   20   15   30   20   40   25   30   miles
kilometres

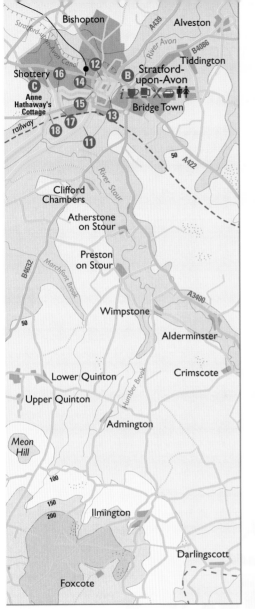

15 TR, SP Shottery. *23km (14.5 miles)*

16 TL at TJ, no SP. To visit Anne Hathaway's Cottage, SO.

To continue main route, TL, SP Bidford. Pass Bell pub on RHS.

17 TR at TJ along Evesham Road, no SP.

18 TL along Luddington Road, SP Luddington.

19 TL at TJ onto B439, SP Bidford/Evesham.

20 TL, SP Welford/Long Marston. Just after Bell Inn on RHS:

21 TR into Church Street, no SP (30.5km/ 19 miles). Bear L along Headland Road.

22 TR at TJ opposite Roseleigh, no SP. Continue through Barton.

23 SO at XR, SP Marcliff/Cleeve Prior/ Badsey (37.5km/23.5 miles). Continue through Cleeve Prior.

24 TL at XR along Arrow Lane, SP North Littleton/Pebworth. Enter North Littleton and just after pub:

25 TR at large grass triangle, no SP, to follow SP for Middle Littleton. After 20m, TR at TJ, no SP. Enter Middle Littleton. (For tithe barn, TR as road bears L.)

26 TL at TJ along B4085, SP South Littleton/Evesham. Just after crossing railway:

27 TL at XR, SP Bretforton.

28 TR at TJ onto B4035, SP Badsey/ Evesham.

29 TL (effectively SO), no SP. Then TL at TJ, no SP, and return to car park to finish the ride.
49.5km (31 miles)

13 TR at TJ opposite war memorial, SP Evesham/Warwick/Birmingham.

14 TL at XR. Immediately TL at TJ, no SP (opposite Twelfth Night B&B). At large roundabout:

Route 14

THE MALVERNS – LEDBURY AND BROMYARD

Route information

Distance 53km (33 miles)

Grade Moderate

Terrain Mostly quiet, undulating lanes and B roads. There is a steep climb to Fromes Hill.

Time to allow 4–5 hours.

Getting there by car Ledbury is 19km (12 miles) east of Hereford at the junction of the A438 and A449. Park in the Lawnside car park, by the swimming pool.

Getting there by train There is a railway station at Ledbury. For travel information telephone (08457) 484950 or visit www.nationalrail.co.uk

A pleasant ride through the Herefordshire countryside, taking in the market towns of Ledbury and Bromyard. The quiet lanes used pass hop fields, orchards and vineyards. There are good views along the way, particularly across the Malvern Hills.

Places of interest along the route

A Ledbury

An old market town with many half-timbered houses. The 17th-century market hall stands on wooden pillars in the market place. The **Butcher Row House Museum**, Church Lane, describes the local history. Open Easter to September, 1100–1700; October open weekends only. Telephone (01531) 632616. For more information on Ledbury, contact the Tourist Information Centre on (01531) 636147 or visit www.ledburyonline.co.uk or www. thisisledbury. co. uk

B Bromyard

Another old market town, on a site by the River Frome occupied since before the compilation of the Domesday Book in 1086. The village has an annual gala and also holds a folk and a musical festival each year. **Bromyard Heritage Centre**, Rowberry Street, has an exhibition on hop cultivation and describes local history. Telephone (01885) 482341. **Bromyard Teddy and Doll Museum** houses a huge collection of old toys, including old teddy bears, Captain Scarlet and other displays of Gerry Anderson's characters. Also Dalek exhibition. Open all year, Monday, Wednesday–Saturday 0930–1700. Charge. Telephone (01885) 488329 or visit www.teddybearsofbromyard.com

C Bosbury Church, Bosbury

The church was built around 1180, next to the Bishop's Palace of Bosbury, of which there are only scant remains. The church tower was built for defence during Welsh raids – the walls are 1.8m (6 feet) thick. The tower's spire was lost in 1638 after a lightening strike. The church contains interesting relics, including a 15th-century rood screen, memorials and 14th-century preaching cross in the churchyard. Contact Ledbury Tourist Information Centre for more details.

Food and drink

There are a number of places for refreshment in Ledbury and Bromyard, a shop and pub in Bishop's Frome and a café in Fromes Hill.

The Wheatsheaf Pub, Fromes Hill
Bar and restaurant meals, B&B.

Cider Orchard

Route description

To start from Ledbury railway station, TL out of station. Continue SO to join route opposite market hall (within direction 1).

To start from Lawnside car park, TR out of car park. TL at TJ into Bye Street.

1 TR at TJ into High Street, no SP but market hall opposite. TL at traffic lights, SP Malvern.

2 TL, SP Coddington. SO at XR, SP Coddington. Climb and descend, with good views of Malvern hills ahead.

3 TR, SP Cradley. *8km (5 miles)*

4 TR at XR with B4220, SP Cradley.

5 TR at TJ, SP Worcester, and take first TL, SP Suckley. Keep R, SP Suckley.

6 TL at TJ, SP Bromyard. Immediately TR, SP Knightwick. *17km (10.5 miles)*

7 TL at XR, SP Linley Green. Climb for good views and keep SO, SP Bromyard.

8 TR at TJ, SP Bromyard B4220. *24km (15 miles)*

9 TL at TJ onto A44, SP Bromyard. Continue into Bromyard.

10 TR, SP Town Centre. TL into one-way street, SP Tourist Information (Bay Horse pub on LHS).

11 To visit Bromyard Heritage Centre, TR at TJ.

Otherwise, TL at TJ, SP Leominster.

12 SO at XR across A44, SP Ledbury B4212. TR at TJ, SP Ledbury A465.

13 Take first TL, SP Ledbury, for good views. Descend to Bishop's Frome (shop in village by Chase Inn pub).

14 TL in Bishop's Frome, SP Acton Beauchamp.

15 TR at TJ, SP Halmond's Frome. Continue SO, SP Fromes Hill, and climb to Fromes Hill.

16 TL at TJ onto A4103, no SP. Immediately TR (by Wheatsheaf Inn), SP Bosbury (café on L, on main road by garage). Descend, with good views of Malvern hills on LHS.

17 TL at TJ, no SP. Continue into Bosbury.

18 TL at TJ onto B4220, no SP (Bosbury church on RHS). TR, SP Wellington Heath.

19 TR at TJ, no SP.

20 TL at TJ, no SP. Continue into Wellington Heath.

21 TR, SP Ledbury.

22 TL at TJ, SP Ledbury B4212.

23 TL at TJ, SP Town Centre. Pass railway station on LHS. SO at traffic light. TR into Bye Street and return to car park to finish the ride.

53km (33 miles)

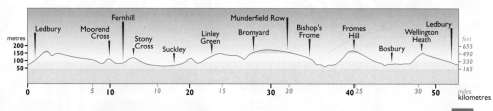

Route 15

NEWPORT AND ECCLESHALL

Route information

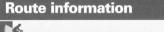

Distance 56km (35 miles)

Grade Easy

Terrain A short stretch of A road, otherwise quiet B and minor roads. The terrain is mostly flat, with just a couple of minor climbs.

Time to allow 3–6 hours.

Getting there by car Newport is 12.5km (8 miles) north east of Wellington at the junction of the A41 and A518, close to the M54, junction 3. Park in the free New Street car park, off the High Street.

Getting there by train There is no railway station at Newport, but the route can be joined from Norton Bridge Station. For travel information telephone (08457) 484950 or visit www.nationalrail.co.uk

From the market town of Newport, on the Shropshire/Staffordshire border, the route heads south to Lilleshall and then east and north, crossing the Shropshire Union Canal, to Gnosall. Continuing north, the route leads to Eccleshall before returning to Newport. There are good views along the way. Cyclists may shorten the route to 45km (28 miles), bypassing Eccleshall. There is also an optional extension of 8km (5 miles) to visit Izaak Walton's Cottage and pass the railway station at Norton Bridge.

Places of interest along the route

A Lilleshall Abbey, Lilleshall

The abbey was founded during the 12th century. Today visitors can see the impressive ruins. Charge. Contact English Heritage to confirm opening times on (01604) 73020 or visit www.english-heritage.org.uk

B Izaak Walton Cottage Museum, Norton Bridge

The museum describes the life of Izaak Walton, author of *The Compleat Angler* in the 17th century. Also herb garden and picnic area. Open April to October, Tuesday–Sunday 1100–1630; November and March, weekends 1100–1600. Charge. Telephone (01785) 619619.

C Bird of Prey Centre, Fletchers Country Garden Centre, Eccleshall

Captive bred birds are displayed here to raise money to help injured birds. The birds were originally taken in by the Gentleshaw Bird of Prey Hospital. After regaining full health birds capable of surviving are released back into the wild. Birds which are permanently disabled but have a good quality of life are paired and the resulting offspring are eventually released back into the wild. The centre offers bird handling courses and flying displays. Café in the garden centre. Telephone (01785) 850379 to confirm opening times.

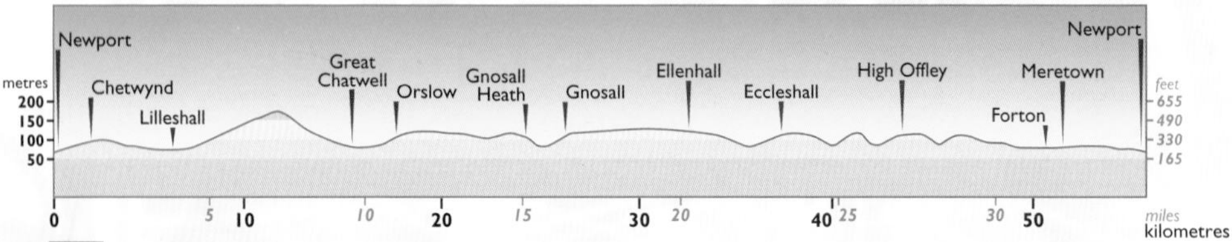

Route description

To start from Norton Bridge railway station, exit station and TR. Continue to direction 20e, to TL at TJ, SP Eccleshall.

To start from New Street car park, Newport, TL out of car park and way 30m along one-way street to High Street. TR at TJ into High Street and SO at mini roundabout.

1 TR into Wellington Road, SP Church Aston.

2 TL, SP Church Aston. Then TL at TJ, no SP. *1.5km (1 mile)*

3 TR at TJ onto A518, SP Telford. SO at roundabout, SP Telford A518.

4 TL at roundabout, SP Lilleshall. Climb to Lilleshall and descend.

5 TL at TJ, SP Lilleshall Abbey. Pass remains of abbey on LHS, then access to Park Cycle Dealers on RHS, along unmade road in Lilleshall Industry Estate (9.5km/6 miles). Continue along this road.

6 TL at TJ, SP National Sports Centre. Take first TR, no SP.

7 Take first TL, no SP.

8 SO at XR over A41. SP Chadwell (CARE here). Pass Chadwell Mill on RHS.

9 TR at TJ, no SP. Cross border into Staffordshire. Continue through Great Chadwell.

10 TL at XR, SP Orslow/High Onn. LHF, SP Orslow (16km/10 miles). Continue through Orslow and keep L, SP High Onn.

11 SO at XR, SP Gnosall. Cross Shropshire Union Canal.

12 TL at TJ, SP Gnosall. Continue into Gnosall.

13 TR at TJ, SP Stafford (Royal Oak pub on LHS).

14 TR at TJ, SP Stafford A518 (24km/ 15 miles). SO (second exit) at mini roundabout into Gnosall, SP village centre (shop on RHS). Cycle through village.

15 TR, SP Ranton. Continue along this road.

16 TL at TJ, no SP.

17 To take short cut, continue on B5405 to TJ with A519.

a TL at TJ, SP Newport. Cross canal and continue through Sutton. Rejoin main route at direction 26, where TR at XR.

To continue main route, TR, SP Ellenhall.

18 TL at TJ, SP Eccleshall (32km/20 miles). Go through Ellenhall.

19 Keep R at grass triangle (immediately before XR at Four Lane Ends). SO at XR, SP Norton Bridge.

20 To visit Izaak Walton's Cottage and return to Norton Bridge station, TR, SP Norton Bridge.

b Take first TR, SP Chebsey.

c Keep L at grass triangle, SP Shallowford. Immediately SO at XR, no SP.

d TR at TJ, no SP, and cross railway. Izaak Walton's cottage on RHS. After visit retrace route over railway (do not TL). Continue SO. Pass Norton Bridge station on RHS.

e TL at TJ, SP Eccleshall. Continue along this road and rejoin main route at direction 20 where SO, SP Eccleshall.

Otherwise, to continue main route, TL at TJ, SP Ecclesall. Pass Bird of Prey Centre on LHS and enter Eccleshall.

21 SO at mini roundabout, SP Loggerheads B5026. Pass Royal Oak pub on LHS.

22 TL, SP Garmelow. SO at XR, SP High Offley (38.5km/24 miles). Continue to Garmelow.

23 SO at XR, SP High Offley. Continue into High Offley.

24 TR at TJ, no SP but opposite church. Take first TL into Pegs Lane, no SP. Cross Shropshire Union Canal (Anchor pub on LHS).

25 TR at TJ, no SP. TL at TJ, no SP. Continue into Forton.

26 SO at XR over A519, no SP (51.5km/ 32 miles). Continue past church and deer park on LHS.

27 TR at TJ onto A518 (CARE), no SP.

28 SO at roundabout (second exit), SP Newport. SO at mini roundabout, no SP.

29 SO at traffic lights, SP Town Centre. TR at mini roundabout into High Street and TL into car park to finish the ride.   ***56km (35 miles)***

Food and drink

Plenty of choice in Newport. There is a pub and store in Gnosall and refreshments are available at the Bird of Prey Centre.

Royal Oak, Gnosall
Open at lunch times.

Anchor, High Offley
By the Shropshire Union Canal. Garden, camping and gift shop.

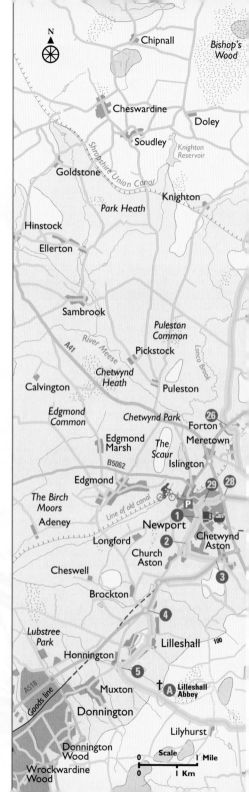

ABBOTS BROMLEY AND CANNOCK CHASE

Route information

 Distance   56km (35 miles)

Grade   Strenuous

Terrain   Minor roads across generally rolling countryside, with a strenuous climb over Cannock Chase.

Time to allow   3–6 hours.

Getting there by car   Abbots Bromley is 9.5km (6 miles) west of Uttoxeter. There is on-street parking in the village.

Getting there by train   There is no railway station in Abbots Bromley. However, the route passes Rugeley Railway Station and the route can be joined there.

This route takes minor roads from Abbots Bromley down to the shore of Blithfield Reservoir and on to the village of Great Haywood, from where it is possible to visit Shugborough Hall. The grounds of the hall are skirted to reach the far side of Cannock Chase. Here the gradient rises and a strenuous climb follows before a super descent into Rugeley. After Rugeley, the route makes a gentle return around the south side of Blithfield Reservoir to return to Abbots Bromley.

Places of interest along the route

Ⓐ Abbots Bromley

An ancient village dating back to 942. Its greatest fame today is the Horn Dance, thought to date back to 1226. The dance takes all day and moves around the village. The actual date of the dance varies each year but is always at the beginning of September. Even on non-dance days, the village is worth a visit. For more information, telephone Burton Tourist Information Centre on (01283) 516609 or visit www.abbotsbromley.com

Ⓑ Shugborough Hall, Great Haywood

The ancestral home of the Earl of Litchfield. It is possible to visit the mansion house, servants' quarters, Park Farm and the gardens. Refreshments available. Open April to September, Tuesday–Sunday 1100–1700. Charge. Telephone (01889) 881388 or visit www.staffordshire.gov.uk/shugboro

Ⓒ Cannock Chase

The area was once the hunting ground of ancient royalty. Today Cannock Chase is a picturesque area of woodland walks, wildlife and superb scenery. Located on the chase are a Commonwealth War Cemetery and the German Military Cemetery containing the graves of 5,000 German Servicemen from two world wars. For more information, telephone Forest Enterprise on (01889) 586593 or visit www.forestry.gov.uk. **The Museum of Cannock Chase** is at Hednesford, quite close to the

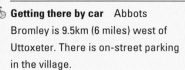

route, on the site of the Valley Colliery. The museum describes local history and has temporary exhibitions and special events. Refreshments available. Open Easter to September, daily 1100–1700; October to Easter, Monday–Friday 1100–1600. Admission free. Telephone (01543) 877666.

Route description

To start from Rugeley Station, exit station and TL to join route at direction 24.

Otherwise, the route starts from the Butter Cross in Baggot Street, Abbots Bromley. TL along Baggot Street.

1 TL into Goose Lane leading to Port Lane, no SP.

2 TR at triangular TJ into Port Lane, no SP.

3 TL at TJ, to join the B5013 and cross Blithfield Reservoir.

4 TL, no SP (second TL after crossing reservoir). Continue SO through Stockwell Heath.

5 TR, no SP (Newlands Lane continues SO). Footpath SP on corner, with a barn entrance opposite turning (6.5km/4 miles). Continue into Colton.

6 TR at mini roundabout into Bellamour Way, SP Rugeley/Colwich.

7 TR at TJ into Colton Road, SP Abbots Bromley/Uttoxeter.

8 TL at triangular junction (where main road takes R bend) into Bellamour Lane, SP Bishton/Stafford.

9 TR at TJ onto A51 (opposite petrol station), SP Stone.

10 TL, SP Colwich/Little Haywood. Descend into Great Haywood.

11 To visit Shugborough Hall, TL (where road takes a R bend outside Clifford Arms). Follow this lane to canalside restaurant and ancient bridge over River Trent. Cross river bridge and back entrance to Shugborough Hall is on RHS.

Otherwise, to continue main route, TR at TJ and continue through Great Haywood.

12 TL at roundabout into Mill Lane, SP Leisure Drive. Follow road through Tixall.

13 TL at obelisk, SP Milford.

17.5km (11 miles)

14 TR at TJ onto A513, no SP but opposite front entrance to Shugborough Hall.

15 TL at roundabout, SP Brockton/Penkridge. Continue into Brockton.

16 TL at triangular junction, SP Village Hall. Immediately TL into Chase Road Brockton.

17 TL at triangular TJ, no SP.

18 SO at XR into Broadhurst Green, no SP.

19 TL at XR into Brindley Road, no SP.

20 TR at TJ into Penkridge Bank, no SP. Continue towards Rugeley.

21 SO at XR (traffic lights) into Church Street, SP Uttoxeter.

22 TR at TJ opposite Chancel Infant School, no SP. TL at roundabout, SP Abbots Bromley.

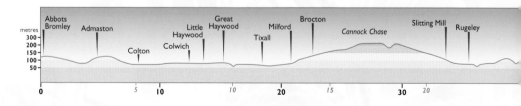

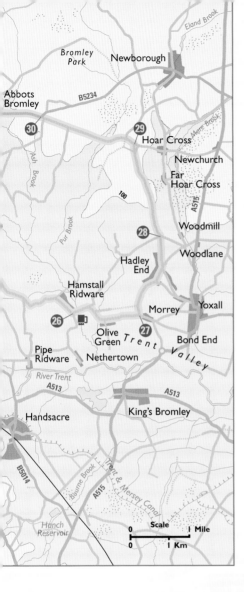

23 SO at roundabout, SP B5013 Abbots Bromley. Pass station and continue under railway.

24 TR opposite Yorkshireman pub, SP Blithbury/Hamstall Ridware.

25 SO at XR by Bull and Spectacles pub, SP Hamstall Ridware/Yoxall.

26 TL into Yoxall Road, SP Morrey/Yoxall/ Burton.

27 TL into Morrey Lane, SP Hadley End/ Dunstall/Hoar Cross.

28 TL at triangular TJ, SP Upper Hoar Cross.

29 TL at TJ, SP Abbots Bromley.

30 TL at TJ, SP Abbots Bromley/Uttoxeter.

31 TR at TJ, SP Uttoxeter, and follow road through Abbots Bromley back to Butter Cross to complete the ride.   *56km (35 miles)*

Food and drink

There are convenience stores in Abbots Bromley, Little Haywood and Great Haywood. There are pubs in most villages passed en route and a canalside restaurant on the Trent and Mersey Canal in Great Haywood. The café at Milford is popular with cyclists and is a useful fuelling point before tackling the climb over Cannock Chase.

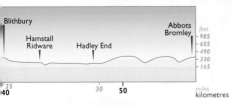

BURTON UPON TRENT AND UTTOXETER

Route information

Distance   64km (40 miles)

Grade   Moderate

Terrain   The first half of the route, as far as Uttoxeter, is almost flat. There is a long climb out of Uttoxeter but the main hills lie after Hoar Cross, as the route climbs up to the Needwood Forest. The section of route after direction 24 can only be described as a roller coaster!

Time to allow   3–6 hours.

Getting there by car   Burton upon Trent is 17.5km (11 miles) south west of Derby on the A38. There are several pay and display car parks in the centre of the town, and there is plenty of free, on-street parking in the side streets near the railway station, the start of the route.

Getting there by train   There is a regular service to Burton upon Trent. For travel information telephone (08457) 484950 or visit www.nationalrail.co.uk

From Burton the route takes a wide loop up the Dove Valley to Uttoxeter. On to Abbots Bromley for a climb through the Needwood Forest before descending back into the Trent Valley.

The bustling brewing town of Burton contrasts with the quiet villages and lanes passed en route. The route follows sections of local designated cycleway and well as part of Sustrans National Cycle Network, NCR 54 which runs between Lichfield and Derby.

Places of interest along the route

Ⓐ Burton upon Trent

Known widely for its brewing industry, which originated in the 13th century. At one time there were 31 breweries producing three million barrels of ale per year. Today only a few remain. The history of the town and of brewing is told at the **Bass Museum**, Horninglow Street. Also preserved steam engine. Café. Open all year, daily 1000–1700. Charge. Telephone (01283) 511000; visit www.bass-museum.com. **Marston's Brewery Visitor Centre**, Shobnall Road, offers brewery tours (must be booked in advance), a visit to the cooperage and beer sampling. Tours available all year, Monday–Friday 1100, 11230 and 1430. Charge. Telephone (01283) 507391. For more information on the town, contact the Tourist Information Centre (TIC) on (01283) 516609.

Ⓑ Tutbury

As Burton is beer, Tutbury is crystal. There are two crystal factories (with shops), **Georgian Crystal**, Silk Mill Lane, telephone (01283) 814534, and **Tutbury Crystal Factory**, Burton Street, telephone (01283) 813281. The other main attraction is **Tutbury Castle**, once Mary, Queen of Scots prison. Tearoom. Open April to September, Wednesday–Sunday and Bank

Holiday Mondays, 1100–1700. Charge. Contact Burton TIC or visit www.tutbury.co.uk for further details.

ⓒ Sudbury Hall, Sudbury

Construction of the hall began in 1660 and it is considered to be one of the most richly decorated English country houses of its time. The architecture is predominantly Jacobean augmented with classical style decoration. The house is complemented by the **Museum of Childhood** with its reconstructed Victorian schoolroom and nursery. Gardens and lakeside walks. Refreshments available. Open April to October, Wednesday–Sunday 1300–1730. Charge. Telephone (01283) 585305.

ⓓ Uttoxeter

A busy market town best known for its National Hunt Steeplechase course. The town itself makes for a good lunch stop.

ⓔ Abbots Bromley

An ancient village dating back to 942. Its claim to fame is the Horn Dance, thought to date back to 1226. See Route 16 for more information.

Food and drink

Plenty of choice in Burton and Uttoxeter. There are several pubs and cafés in Tutbury and Abbots Bromley has several pubs and convenience stores. Refreshments are also available at the Bass Museum, Tutbury Castle, Tutbury Crystal Factory and Sudbury Hall.

🄿 Red Cow Pub, near Uttoxeter
Passed on the route, on the B5013. Bar meals available.

🄿 Maynell Ingram Arms, Hoar Cross
✕ *This hotel offers bar and restaurant meals.*

Route description

TR out of railway station car park. Go down the hill to join Station Street by the Roebuck pub. TL at XR (traffic lights). To visit Bass Museum TL at TJ (traffic lights). Otherwise, to follow main route, TR at TJ.

1 TL at XR (traffic lights) by Queens Hotel. Bear left along Wetmoor Road, past SP 3T weight restriction. Where all through traffic is SP to TL, follow cycle path SO. Continue along cycle path, SP Stretton, passing The Great Northern Pub along a residential street. Bear L at Plasplugs and cross railway bridge. Follow cycle path around R of roundabout (CARE), SP Stretton, and to its end in Beech Drive, Stretton.
4km (2.5 miles)

2 TL at TJ at end of Beech Drive. Then TR at TJ. TL into The Green, SP Parking (before Victoria Wines). Then TL at TJ in front of Bridge Cottages.

3 TR, SP Rolleston.

4 TR at TJ into Beacon Road, SP Rolleston/Tutbury.

5 TL into Chapel Lane, SP Tutbury. TL at TJ, no SP.

6 TR into Corn Mill Lane, no SP (but main road continues to L, SP Uttoxeter/Tutbury). Continue into Tutbury.

7 TR at TJ into High Street, no SP. Follow High Street into Lower High Street and bear R into Bridge Street, SP Station.

8 SO at roundabout, SP Uttoxeter/Hatton.

9 Cross the level crossing and TL at mini roundabout into Scropton Road, SP Scropton.

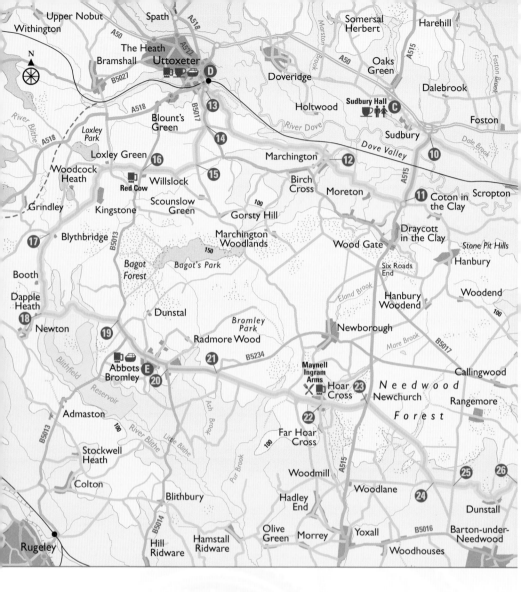

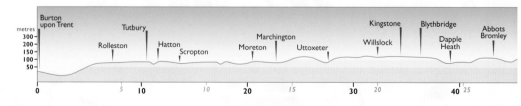

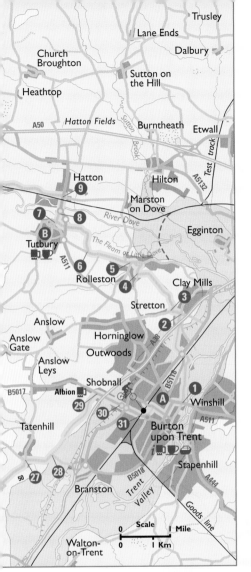

10 To visit Sudbury, TR at TJ onto A515, SP Sudbury/Doveridge (16.5km/10.5 miles). Immediately TL into minor road (called Main Road). Follow this road into Sudbury.

Otherwise, TL at TJ onto A515, SP Lichfield/Scropton/Draycott in the Clay/Kings Bromley.

11 TR at roundabout into Mordon Lane, SP Marchington. Continue into Marchington.

12 TR at TJ, no SP. Pass village hall on LHS and St Peters School on RHS. Continue through village and keep L at junction in front of hall. Bear R into Moisty Lane. Follow this road for approximately 3km (2 miles) and descend carefully around LH bend towards Uttoxeter Race Course.

13 To visit Uttoxeter, SO at mini roundabout into Old Knotty Way, SP Uttoxeter. Immediately TR at roundabout, SP Town Centre – pavement on LHS becomes cycle path here. Follow this over railway bridge and TL at next roundabout to access Uttoxeter town centre (27km/17 miles).

Otherwise, to follow main route, TL at mini roundabout into Highwood Road, SP Marchington. Climb away from Uttoxeter.

14 TR at XR, SP Scounslow Green.

15 TR at XR, SP Loxley/Kingstone/Stafford.

16 SO at XR over B5013, SP Kingstone.

17 TL (before bridge over beck), SP Newton/Admaston (post box on RHS).

37km (23 miles)

18 TL, SP Abbots Bromley.

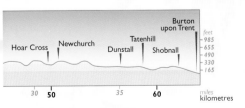

19 TR onto B5013, SP Abbots Bromley/Lichfield. Continue through Abbots Bromley.

20 TL into Ashbrook Lane, SP Hoar Cross/Newborough.

21 TR, SP Hoar Cross.

22 SO at XR (Maynell Ingram Arms here), SP Needwood/Barton. Climb steep hill past Jacksons Bank, a Duchee of Lancaster woodland.

23 SO at XR onto Scotch Hill, SP Scotch Hill/Barton-under-Needwood.

24 TL at XR, SP Dunstall/Tatenhill.

25 SO at XR, SP Dunstall.

26 TL at triangular junction, SP Tatenhill/Anslow, and join NCR 54.

27 TR at XR, SP Branston/Burton/NCR 54.

28 As road turns R, TL to follow farm road through Lawns Farm (effectively SO). SP Private Road can be seen but this is part of NCR 54.

29 TR at TJ (where farm road comes out by Albion pub).

30 TL (effectively SO) at roundabout, SP Town Centre. SO at next roundabout (busy) and immediately bear R onto cycle path which dives under railway line.

31 TL at TJ (effectively SO), opposite MG garage. TL into Cross Street. TL at TJ into Station Street and return to station to finish the ride.

64km (40 miles)

Sudbury Hall

BRIDGNORTH AND THE SEVERN VALLEY

Route information

 Distance 66.5km (41.5 miles)

 Grade Moderate

 Terrain Quiet lanes and B roads, through mainly arable farm land.

Time to allow 4–6 hours.

Getting there by car Bridgnorth is 19km (12 miles) west of Wolverhampton, at the junction of the A458 and A454. Park in the Smithfield long stay car park in the centre of town, behind Somerfield supermarket.

 Getting there by train Bridgnorth and Highley (passed en route) are on the Severn Valley Steam Railway (see below for details) which can be joined at Kidderminster. For details of the main line service to Kidderminster, telephone (08457) 484950 or visit www.nationalrail.co.uk

A pleasant ride offering excellent views across Shropshire. There is an optional short cut, but cyclists could cycle as far as Highley and return via the steam railway, or, put the bike on the steam railway at Bridgnorth and start from Highley, missing the hilly B4555.

Route description

TL out of car park then keep R. TL at mini roundabout, no SP. Pass bike shop on RHS.

1 TR into High Street, no SP. TL at XR (opposite Museum of Childhood) into Cartway,

SP One Way. Descend and TR at TJ beside river.

2 TR at TJ, no SP. Then TR at TJ, SP Severn Valley Railway.

3 TL, SP Highley. TL again, SP Highley B4555. Follow River Severn and pass Daniel's Mill on RHS. Climb through Eardington and Chelmarsh for good views across Chelmarsh Reservoir. Pass Bulls Head PH on RHS. Climb gradually to Highley. Pass Jays Café and village shops.

4 SO at mini roundabout, no SP.

13km (8 miles)

5 To visit Severn Valley Railway and Severn Valley Country Park (adds extra 2km/1 mile), TL into Station Road. Descend and TR for country park; SO for railway.

Otherwise, to continue main route, TR, SP Netherton. Then, TL, SP Borle Mill. Descend, cross stream and climb to TJ with B4555.

6 TR at TJ, SP Cleobury Mortimer.

7 TR at TJ, SP Bridgnorth B4368 (16km/ 10 miles). Good views from ridge. Descend through woodland.

8 TL to visit Rays Farm.

To continue route, climb to Deuxhill.

9 To take short cut, SO, SP Bridgnorth. Continue into Bridgnorth and TL at TJ. Rejoin outward route at direction 3 and retrace route to car park to finish the ride.

Otherwise, to continue main route, TL, SP The Down.

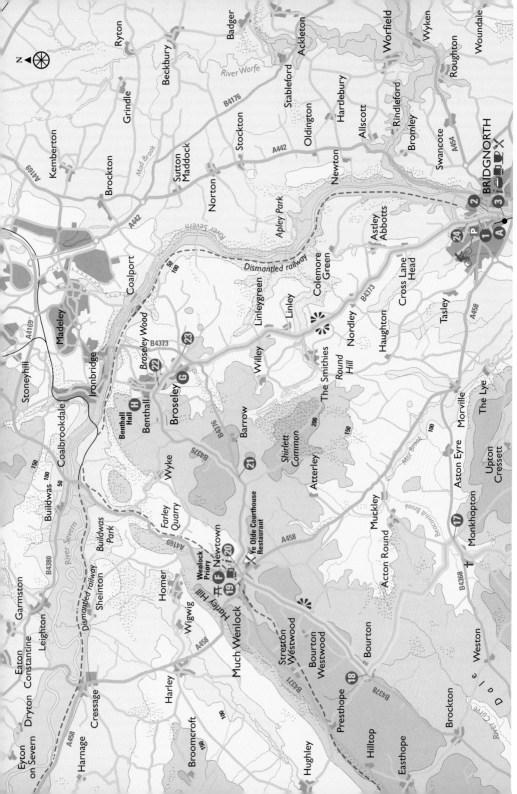

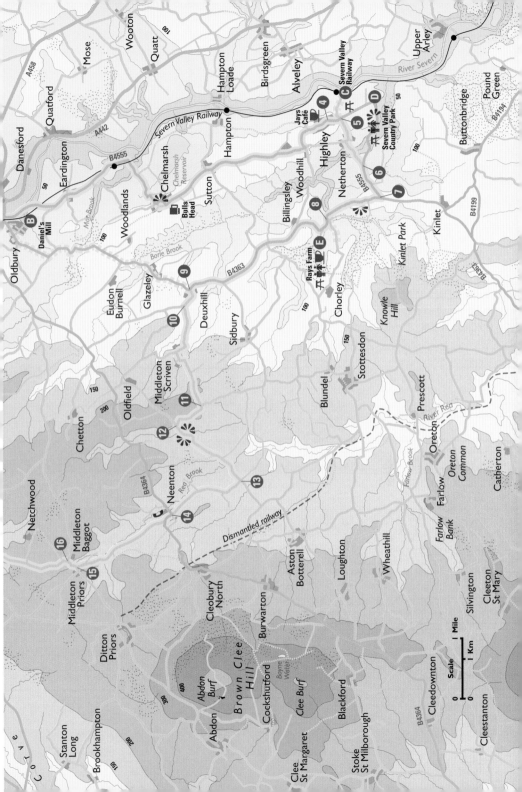

10 TL, SP Middleton Scriven (23km/14.5 miles). Continue through Middleton Scriven.

11 TR at TJ, SP Oldfield.

12 TL at TJ, SP Walkerslow. Gradually climb for views L across Brown Clee Hill.

13 TR at XR, SP Neenton, and descend into Neenton.

14 TL at TJ, SP Ludlow (32km/20 miles). TR, no SP but by telephone box.

15 TR at TJ, SP Bridgnorth. Climb.

16 TL, SP Monkhopton. Descend through woodland into Monkhopton. TR at TJ opposite church, no SP. Then TR at TJ, SP Bridgnorth B4368.

17 TL at XR, SP Much Wenlock (40km/25 miles). Climb into Bourton.

18 TR at TJ, SP Much Wenlock. Gradually climb for panoramic views across Shropshire. Continue on this road for descent to Much Wenlock.

19 TR at TJ, no SP (49.5km/31 miles). LHF (apparent SO), SP Abbey Ruins. Pass restaurant on RHS.

20 To visit Wenlock Priory, TL at TJ.

Otherwise, to continue route, TR at TJ (Tourist Information on LHS), SP Broseley.

21 Keep L, SP Broseley. Pass entrance to Benthall Hall on LHS, SP Benthall Hall. Descend then climb into Brosely.

22 SO at mini roundabout into High Street, no SP. SO at next mini roundabout, SP Ironbridge.

23 TR at XR, SP Bridgnorth (56km/35 miles). Gradually climb for panoramic views across Shropshire and Staffordshire. Descend then climb into Bridgnorth. Cycle through gate house.

24 TR (before Old Town Hall), SP Shrewsbury. Retrace outward route back to car park to finish the ride. *66.5km (41.5 miles)*

Places of interest along the route

A Bridgnorth

The town is split into the High Town (town centre) on the cliff top and the Low Town across the River Severn. A **cable railway** connects the two. The railway is the oldest and steepest funicular in the country, offering great views across Shropshire. Open summer, Monday–Saturday 0800–2000, Sunday 1200–2000; winter 0800–1830, Sunday 1200–1830. Charge. Bridgnorth has many interesting old buildings, a Museum of Costume and Childhood and a local history museum. Contact the Tourist

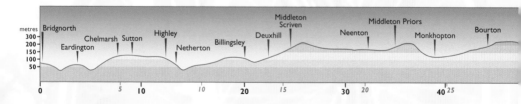

Information Centre for information on (01746) 763257 or visit www.bridgnorth.shropshire.com

B Daniel's Mill, Oldbury

A restored water mill. The wheel powers a corn mill producing traditional flour. Guided tours. Open Easter to September, Wednesday, Saturday (not during September), Sunday 1400–1800; Bank Holidays 1100–1800. Charge. Telephone (01746) 762753.

C Severn Valley Railway, Highley

The railway offers a 25.5km (16 mile) journey along the Severn Valley, from Bridgnorth to Highley and on to Bewdley and Kidderminster. Refreshments available. Open May to September, daily; October to April, weekends only. Telephone (01299) 403816 or visit www.svr.co.uk

D Severn Valley Country Park, Highley

The country park comprises a large area of the Severn Valley. Visitor centre, waymarked walks and direct access to the Severn Valley railway. Free admission to park. Visitor centre open March to October, Wednesday–Sunday 1200–1700; November to March 1100–1600. Telephone (01746) 781192.

E Rays Farm, Billingsley

Home to lots of animals and birds, including squirrels, deer and over 50 owls. Woodland walks, wood carving trail. Indoor and outdoor picnic areas and tearoom. Open March to December, daily 1000–1730 (dusk in winter). Charge. Telephone (01299) 841255.

F Wenlock Priory, Much Wenlock

The substantial remains of a priory, with 12th-century carvings, lawns and ornamental topiary. English Heritage property. Open April to October, daily 1000–1800; November to March, Wednesday–Sunday 1000–1600. Telephone (01952) 727466.

G Broseley

A medieval town centred on its church. In the early 17th century, the town was a thriving industrial development and a major centre for mining and manufacture of ceramic wares, bricks and clay pipes. A town trail describes the many interesting historic buildings. Telephone the library/information point for more information on (01952) 884900.

H Benthall Hall, Broseley

This stone house contains an impressive oak staircase and elaborate plaster ceiling. There are collections of furniture, ceramics and paintings. Garden. National Trust property. Open April to September, Wednesday, Sunday and Bank Holidays 1330–1730. Telephone (01952) 882159.

Food and drink

There is a wide choice of places to eat in Bridgnorth. There is a café in Highley and a café and a pub in Much Wenlock.

Much Wenlock	Broseley	Linleygreen	Bridgnorth	feet
				985
				655
				490
				330
				165

| 30 | 50 | 35 | 60 | 40 | miles kilometres |

STAFFORD AND WEDGWOOD

Route information

Distance 72.5km (45 miles)

Grade Moderate

Terrain The road surface is tarmac, other than a section of cycle path along the disused railway line in and out of Stafford, and the woodland track used to descend between Swynnerton Old Park and the A34. The southern end of the route is gently graded but the northern end is quite hilly, with a long climb up into Swynnerton Old Park.

Time to allow 3–8 hours.

Getting there by car Stafford is 22.5km (14 miles) south of Stoke-on-Trent. There is plenty of parking around the town centre. The route starts from the railway station.

Getting there by train There is a regular service to Stafford Station. For travel information telephone (08457) 484950 or visit www.nationalrail.co.uk

Places of interest along the route

Ⓐ Millmeece Pumping Station, Millmeece

A preserved pumping station with two horizontal steam engines. The station formerly supplied water to Newcastle-under-Lyme and Stoke-on-Trent. Open most Sundays. Charge. Telephone for dates of steaming on (01270) 87368 or (01785) 617171.

Ⓑ Wedgwood Visitor Centre, Wedgwood

The visitor centre tells the history of Wedgwood pottery and offers a tour of the factory to see how the latest technology is used to make the current range of pottery. Shop and restaurant. Open all year, Monday–Friday 0900–1700, weekends 1000– 1700 (shop closes 1600 on Sunday). Charge (restaurant access free). Telephone (01782) 204218; www.thewedgwoodstory.com

Ⓒ Izaak Walton's Cottage, Norton Bridge

Izaak Walton wrote *The Compleat Angler* in 1653. The cottage was eventually left to Stafford Corporation and is now restored and open to the public. See route 3 for more information.

The route heads out of Stafford on a cycle path along a disused railway line before turning north along quiet lanes, past Millmeece Pumping Station. The middle section of the route is the most hilly, as it leads to the Wedgwood estate and the visitor centre. The final section takes cyclists through Stone and past Izaak Walton's cottage, before returning to Stafford along the cycle path.

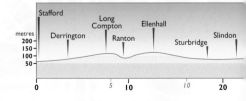

Route description

Exit Stafford station and TL. TL at first round-about. TR into Peel Street. TL at TJ then TL at XR into Castle Street. Cross railway bridge. Follow cycle path and TR at TJ, SP Cycle Path Derrington. SO at roundabout and continue to end of road. TR onto cycle path, SP Private Road/Pedestrianised Access Only. Access parallel cycle path after 100m and follow it to:

1 TL at Red Lion pub. Go through pub car park and TR onto road.

2 TL at TR, SP Haughton/Gnosall.

3 TR at TJ, SP Ranton/Eccleshall.

4 Continue along main road into Dog Lane, SP Ranton/Eccleshall.

5 RHF along Brook Lane.

6 SO at XR across B5405, SP Ellenhall/Eccleshall.

7 RHF, SP Eccleshall.

8 SO at XR, SP Norton Bridge/Stone.

9 TR at TJ, SP Norton Bridge/Stone. Cross bridge then TL at XR, SP Slindon/Millmeece.

10 SO at XR, SP Slindon/Newcastle.

11 SO at staggered XR, SP Brocton/Croxton. Descend and cross stream. Pass large farm on RHS:

12 TR, no SP.

13 RHF, no SP. Cross beck.

14 TR at TJ opposite church, no SP. TL into Sytch Lane. Cross railway line and:

15 TR at TJ onto A519. TL into Mill Meece Marsh, SP Millmeece Steam Engines. Pass pumping station on RHS.

16 SO at XR, SP Hatton/Cranberry/Stableford. After Cranberry:

17 TL down minor road (before farm on RHS), no SP. Cross railway line and continue to Chapel Chorlton.

18 RHF at church then RHF at village green.

19 TR at TJ onto A51, SP Stone/Stafford/M6.

20 SO (where A51 turns R, after crossing railway line), SP Hanchurch/Trentham. Climb up into Swynnerton Old Park until:

21 TR into parking area, opposite Forestry Commission Swynnerton Old Park SP. Take LHF at a grass roundabout in car park. Cycle along gravel road. Take LHF past gate to Hanchurch Severn Trent Water site. Descend wooded track to join metalled road leading down to:

22 TR at TJ onto A519, no SP. After crossing a bridge:

23 TR, no SP. Follow road to R and under A519. Take LHF.

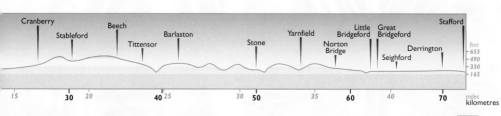

24 TL at TJ, no SP.

25 TR onto A34, SP Stone/Stafford. Descend hill and:

26 TL into Tittensor Road, SP Barlaston/ Wedgwood. Follow road through Barlaston, cross railway line and climb hill to:

27 TL into Longton Road, SP Wedgwood/ Blurton.

28 TL as road bears R, SP Wedgwood.

29 TL at TJ, SP Visitors. Visitor centre is on RHS (41.5km/26 miles). TR on leaving the visitor centre and continue towards Wedgwood Station. Cross railway line via pedestrian crossing (vehicle crossing is only open for a limited period each day).

30 TL at TJ, no SP.

31 SO at XR, SP Meaford.

32 TL, no SP, and almost immediately cross canal. TR at TJ between canal and railway line, no SP.

33 TR into Margaret Street and TR at TJ, no SP. Pass under railway bridge then:

34 TL, no SP.

35 TL at TJ onto A34 and immediately TR by Walton Inn.

36 TL at TJ, SP Norton Bridge.

37 TR at roundabout, SP Eccleshall. Continue and cross railway line.

38 TL, SP Norton Bridge/Great Bridgeford. Pass Izaak Walton's cottage on LHS after approximately 1.5km (1 mile).

39 TL at TJ onto A5013, SP Great Bridgeford/Stafford.

40 Before crossing railway line, TR into Newport Road, SP Village Hall/Gliding Club.

41 TL, SP Sleighford/Doxey. Continue to pass large farm on LHS and:

42 TL, no SP. Arrive ford SP Unsuitable for Motor Vehicles. Cross ford via footbridge.

43 TL at TJ, no SP.

44 TR at TJ, SP Derrington/Haughton.

45 TL into Blackhole Lane, SP Derrington.

46 TL into Red Lion pub car park. TR along cycle path into Stafford. When the cycle path ends, join parallel road on RHS, SP Town Centre. SO at roundabout, no SP. TL just before next roundabout, SP Cycle Way/Town Centre. Cross railway bridge into Railway Street and take sharp right (opposite Railway Inn). TR (effectively SO) as road bears L, and return to station to finish the ride.

72.5km (45 miles)

Food and drink

There is plenty of choice for refreshment in Stafford and Stone. Cranberry and Barlaston have convenience stores and there are pubs in Millmeece, Cranberry, Stableford, Barlaston, Seighford and Derrington. Refreshments are also available at the Wedgwood Visitor Centre.

BEWDLEY AND THE WYRE FOREST

Route information

 Distance 78.5km (49 miles)

Grade Moderate

Terrain B roads and quiet lanes. There is one long climb up Cleehill.

Time to allow 5–7 hours.

Getting there by car Bewdley is 5km (3 miles) west of Kidderminster, off the A456. The route starts from Gardens Meadow long stay car park, off Lax Lane and Severn Side South (by the River Severn).

Getting there by train The nearest railway station is at Kidderminster. For travel information telephone (08457) 484950 or visit www.nationalrail.co.uk

A scenic ride which uses a mixture of B roads and quiet lanes. From Bewdley, the route follows the Teme Valley before ascending Cleehill for outstanding views across the Heart of England to the Brecon Beacons. The route then descends and follows attractive lanes through the Wyre Forest back to Bewdley. The main attraction along the route is the scenery – Cleehill, the Severn and Teme Valleys, the Wyre Forest and, in Spring, the apple orchards in blossom.

Places of interest along the route

Ⓐ Bewdley

A small town situated on the River Severn. The town contains some fine Georgian buildings and was the birthplace of Stanley Baldwin, three times British prime minister. **Bewdley Museum**, Load Street, describes the town's history through many displays. There are daily demonstrations of rope and clay pipe manufacture. Resident crafts people, herb garden and picnic area. Open daily, April to September 1100–1700; October 1100–1600. Charge. Telephone (01299) 403573.

Route description

To start from Kidderminster Railway Station, join A449 and head north, SP Wolverhampton/Stourbridge. TL onto B4189 and soon TL onto B4190. Follow this road across River Severn and into Bewdley.

To start from Bewdley, TR out of car park. TL at TJ onto B4190 and enter town. Keep L of church in centre of Load Street and TL, SP Ribbesford/Country Park. Stay on this road to climb out of town, descend and follow River Severn.

1 SO at XR, SP Shrawley B4196.

2 TR at TJ, SP Shrawley B4196. Cycle through Astley Cross and pass memorial to

Bewdley

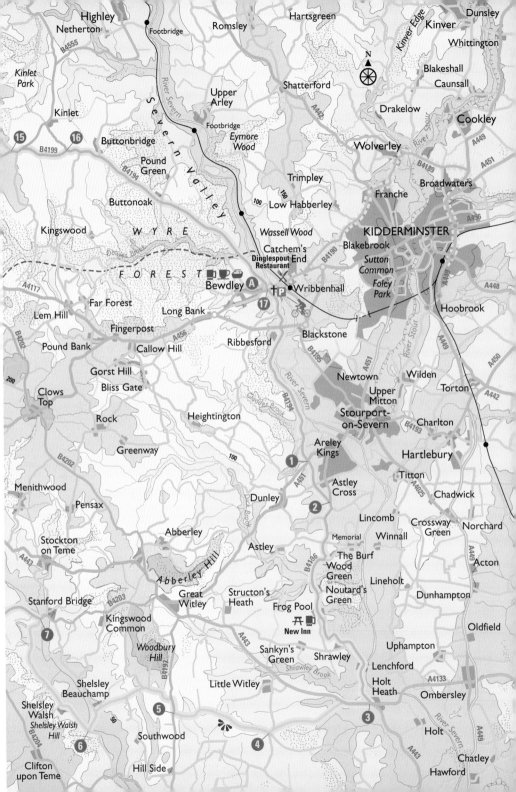

Stanley Baldwin on LHS. Pass Shrawley picnic site and New Inn pub on RHS (9km/5.5 miles). Continue into Holt Heath.

3 TR at TJ, SP Tenbury A443. Take first TL, SP Ockeridge.

4 TR at XR, SP Marley Hill Side (17.5km/ 11 miles). Pass through apple orchards. Good views of Malvern Hills on LHS.

5 TR at TJ, SP Great Witley B4197. Take first TL, SP Shelsley Beauchamp and continue through this village.

6 TR at TJ, SP Shelsley Walsh.

25km (15.5 miles)

7 TL at TJ, SP Bromyard B4203. Take first TR, SP Orleton. Enter Teme Valley.

30.5km (19 miles)

8 TL, SP Highwood (SP in hedge). Do **NOT** descend to river! Continue towards Tenbury Wells.

9 TR at grass triangle, SP Tenbury. Descend into Tenbury Wells, passing old pump house on RHS after bridge.

10 TR at TJ in Tenbury Wells, no SP (44km/27.5 miles). Cross River Teme.

11 TL at TJ, SP Ludlow A456. TR, SP Cleehill B4214. Continue for long climb to Cleehill village, with good views on LHS.

12 TR at TJ in Cleehill, SP Bewdley A4117 (53km/33 miles). NB: toilets on LHS, view point on RHS – enjoy the outstanding views across Worcestershire and Herefordshire as far as the Brecon Beacons. Continue on this road for long, gradual descent.

13 TL, SP Oreton.

14 TL at TJ, SP Bagginswood. After short, steep descent, TR at TJ, SP Bagginswood (62.5km/39 miles). Continue towards Bewdley.

15 TL at TJ, SP Bewdley B4194. Take second TR, SP B4194 Bewdley.

16 Pass through Buttonbridge and enter Wyre Forest (73km/45.5 miles). Continue through forest on B4194 into Bewdley.

17 TL into Load Street (church on RHS in centre of road). Continue along Load Street to River Severn. TR into car park to finish the ride.

78.5km (49 miles)

Food and drink

Plenty of choice in Bewdley and Tenbury Wells. There is a pub near Shrawley.

Teme Bridge, Tenbury Wells

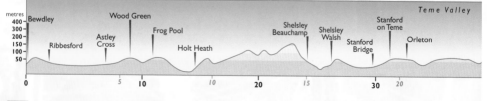

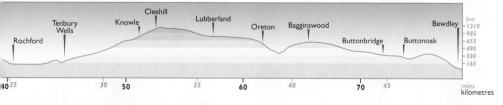

Rochford · Tenbury Wells · Knowle · Cleehill · Lubberland · Oreton · Bagginswood · Buttonbridge · Buttonoak · Bewdley

feet
1310
985
655
490
330
165

miles
kilometres

Route information

 Distance 87km (54 miles)

 Grade Easy

 Terrain Tarmac roads throughout. One short, steep climb. Quiet lanes on the outward section and busier A roads for the return via Ruby.

 Time to allow 6–9 hours.

Getting there by car Warwick is 14.5km (9 miles) south west of Coventry and is best accessed from the M40, following SP Town Centre, where there is parking. The route starts from the railway station.

 Getting there by train There is a frequent service to Warwick. For travel information telephone (08457) 484950 or visit www.nationalrail.co.uk

Starting from Warwick, the route heads through the flat countryside to the south east of the town. One of the better viewpoints in the area is the country park at Burton Dassett and it is to here that the route climbs for expansive views. The subsequent route follows the valley in which the Oxford Canal was built, with quiet lanes linking the pretty villages of Priors Hardwell and Marston Doles. Although the canal is rarely seen it can be easily accessed at Napton on the Hill. The route then follows the A426 to access Rugby and main roads are

used from here to return to Warwick. If you wish to reduce the total mileage, it would be worth returning west to Warwick from just before Rugby.

Route description

Exit Warwick railway station. TR at TJ opposite Volvo garage, no SP.

1 TR at TJ (traffic lights), SP Town Centre/ Stratford/Birmingham. Pass museum on LHS. Bear L, following one-way street.

2 TL at roundabout, SP Birmingham/ Banbury/Stratford/Barford.

3 SO at roundabout, SP Birmingham/ Banbury.

4 TL, SP Whitnash/Harbury.

5 SO at XR (roundabout), SP Bishop's Tachbrook/Harbury.

6 SO at XR (roundabout), SP Bishop's Tachbrook/Harbury.

7 SO at XR, SP Harbury.

8 SO at XR, SP Harbury/Bishop's Itchington.
8km (5 miles)

9 TR, SP Bishop's Itchington.

10 TR at TJ opposite garage, no SP. TL along Knightcote Road, SP Knightcote/Fenny Compton. Enter Knightcote.

Warwick Castle

11 TR at TJ, SP Leisure Drive.

19km (12 miles)

12 TL, SP Northend.

13 TL at TJ, no SP (Red Lion pub on LHS).

14 TL at TJ, SP Burton Hills. Continue along this road, passing country park on LHS.

15 TL at XR, SP Fenny Compton.

24km (15 miles)

16 TL at TJ, SP Wormleighton.

17 TL at TJ, SP Wormleighton/Banbury.

18 TR at TJ, SP Wormleighton. Then TL, SP Wormleighton. Continue through Wormleighton.

19 TL, SP Priors Hardwick.

30.5km (19 miles)

20 TL, SP Village Centre.

21 TL at TJ, SP Napton/Southam.

22 TL at TJ just before bridge, SP Napton/Southam.

23 TR, no SP.

24 TR at TJ (effectively SO), SP Napton/Stockton.

25 SO at XR, SP Tounlow/Stockton/Broadwell.

41km (25.5 miles)

26 TR at XR along A426, SP Dunchurch/Rugby.

27 SO at XR, SP Rugby (54km/33.5 miles). Follow SP to Rugby across more roundabouts. As you approach town centre, follow SP Leamington A4071.

28 SO at roundabout, SP London/Coventry (there is a brief cycleway that goes to LHS of roundabout).

29 TL, SP Princethorpe. *46.5km (29 miles)*

30 TL at TJ, SP Princethorpe.

31 TR at TJ, then TL, SP Leamington/Coventry.

71.5km (44.5 miles)

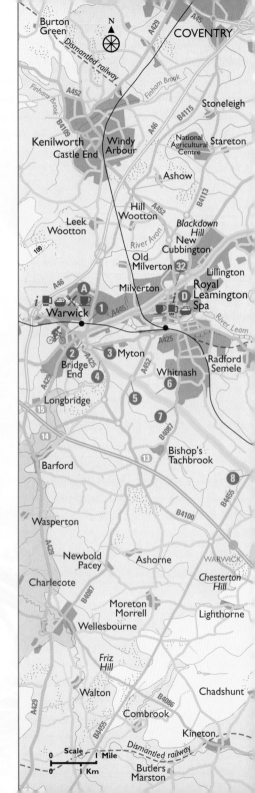

32 SO at XR, SP Leamington. Continue to follow SP Warwick. When close to centre of Warwick, TR along Coventry Road, SP Coventry, and TL to return to the station and the end of the ride. **87km (54 miles)**

Places of interest along the route

A Warwick

As the county town of Warwickshire, Warwick is often referred to as the Heart of England – it is the meeting point of many roads. It is dominated by the medieval **Castle**, Castle Hill, built by the Beauchamps who were the first Earls of Warwick. The castle is well-preserved and features an armoury, dungeon and torture chamber. It was home to Richard Neville, the so-called Kingmaker. In 1461 he replaced Henry VI with his son Edward IV, but subsequently fell out with Edward and brought Henry back from France. The castle grounds were laid out by Capability Brown. Open all year, daily 1000–1800; November to March closes 1700. Charge. Telephone (01926) 406600. Other museums and architecture illustrate Warwick's illustrious past. These include the **Market Hall Museum**, Market Place, which houses exhibitions on archaeology and history. Open May to September, Monday–Saturday 1000–1700, Sunday 1430–1700. Admission free. Telephone (01926) 412500. In 1571, the Earl of Leicester founded **Lord Leycester Hospital**, High Street. The chapel, courtyard and guildhall are impressive and the guildhall contains a military museum. Also restored gardens. Open all year, Tuesday–Sunday and Bank Holiday Mondays 1000–1700 (winter closes 1600). Charge. Telephone (01926) 491422. **Oken's House and Doll Museum**, Castle Street, comprises a superb collection of early dolls, housed in one of the few timber buildings that survived

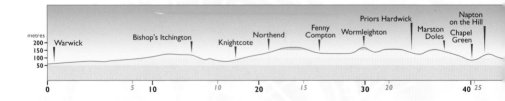

Warwick's great fire of 1694. Open Easter to October, Monday–Saturday 1000–1700, Sunday 1300–1700; November to Easter, Saturday only 1000–dusk. Telephone (01926) 412500. Contact the Tourist Information Centre (TIC) for more information on (01926) 492212.

Ⓑ Burton Dassett Hills Country Park, Burton Dassett

The park comprises around 40.5ha (100 acres) of mostly open hillside offering superb views. It is possible to walk to several elevated points, including Bonfire and Gallows Hills, to admire the surrounding area. Free access at all reasonable times. For further information contact Warwickshire County Parks Information Office on (01827) 872660.

Ⓒ Rugby

Primarily a manufacturing town, Rugby came to prominence when William Webb Ellis ran with a soccer ball in 1823 and so started rubgy football. **The Rugby School Museum**, Little Church Street, describes the school's history. Open all year, daily 1030–1630. Charge. Telephone (01788) 574117. The **James Gilbert Rugby Football Museum**, St Matthews Street, was founded by the nephew of William Gilbert, who made the shoes and boots for Rubgy School. Open all year, Monday–Friday 1000–1700, Saturday 1000–1400. Admission free. Telephone (01788) 542426. Contact the TIC for more details on (01788) 535348.

Ⓓ Royal Leamington Spa

Situated on the River Leam, Leamington Spa grew to prominence as a spa town. In 1838, Queen Victoria visited the town and it gained its Royal suffix. The spa is fed from natural springs and is used for treating rheumatic complaints. It is possible to taste the waters in the pump room. The town's assembly rooms contain an **Art Gallery and Museum** where visitors can see British, Dutch and Flemish paintings of the 16th and 17th centuries, and collections of modern art, pottery, porcelain and 18th-century drinking glasses. Open all year, Wednesday, Friday and Saturday 1030–1700, Tuesday and Thursday 1330–2000, Sunday 1100–1600. Admission free. Telephone (01926) 742700. For more information contact the TIC on (01926) 742762.

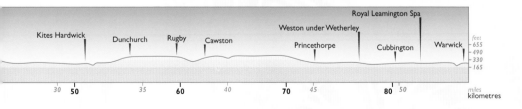

NEWPORT AND CANNOCK CHASE

Route information

 Distance   101km (63 miles)

 Grade   Moderate

Terrain   Generally quiet lanes and B roads, with a couple of short stretches of A road.

Time to allow   5–7 hours.

Getting there by car   Newport is 12.5km (8 miles) north east of Wellington, close to the junction of the A41 and A518. The route starts from the New Street free car park, off the High Street.

 Getting there by train   The route can be easily started from the railway station at Norton Bridge, between Stone and Eccleshall. For travel information telephone (08457) 484950 or visit www.nationalrail.co.uk

An interesting ride which explores the Shropshire and Staffordshire countryside. From Newport, the route passes through mixed farmland to Weston Park, the 17th-century home of the Earls of Bradford. On for a climb to Cannock Chase, a designated Area of Outstanding Natural Beauty, for excellent views as far as Wales. The route continues through the Trent Valley to return to Newport via Stone and Eccleshall. The route crosses the Trent and Mersey, and Shropshire Union Canals. A shorter option is given within the route.

Route description

To start from Norton Bridge Station, TR out of station and through village. TL at TJ, SP Eccleshall, and join route at direction 40.

To start from Newport, TL out of New Street car park, and walk 30m along one-way street to High Street. TR at TJ into High Street. SO at mini roundabout, no SP.

1   SO at roundabout, SP Chetwynd Aston.

2   TR at TJ, SP Wolverhampton A41.

3   TL, SP Great Chatwell. To take optional short cut, SO, SP Moreton.

a   TR at TJ, SP Moreton, and keep SO, SP Church Eaton.

b   SO at XR, SP Church Eaton. Cross canal into Church Eaton.

c   Continue through Church Eaton. Keep R by church, SP Penkridge. TL, SP Woollaston.

d   TL at TJ, SP Penkridge. Continue to outskirts of Penkridge and rejoin route at direction 14.

To follow main route, immediately TR, SP Great Chatwell. Continue into Great Chatwell. Good views across Shropshire on RHS.

4   TR in Great Chatwell, SP Weston-under-Lizard.

5   Continue SO at fork, SP Weston (8km/ 5 miles). Keep L, SP Weston.

6 TR at XR, SP Weston-under-Lizard.

7 SO at XR (across A5, Watling Street), SP Tong. Pass entrance to Weston Park on LHS. Cycle through woodland beside park.

8 TL at XR, SP Brewood. *15km (9.5 miles)*

9 SO at XR, no SP. *20km (12.5 miles)*

10 TR at TJ in Bishops Wood, SP Brewood. Continue into Brewood.

11 Cross canal (tearoom on R in village). Descend and TL into Vicarage Road, no SP.
25km (15.5 miles)

12 Cross River Penk. SO, SP Penkridge, for gradual climb with good views on LHS.

13 TR at TJ onto A5 (CARE). Immediately TL, SP Water Eaton. Continue to outskirts of Penkridge.

14 NB: optional short cut can be reversed from here to return to Newport.

To follow main route, TR at TJ, SP Penkridge. Pass under railway into town town centre.

15 TR at TJ onto A449, no SP (to visit tearoom, WC or cycle shop, immediately TL).
33km (20.5 miles)

16 TL opposite Railway pub, no SP. Continue through Penkridge.

17 TL at mini roundabout, SP Cannock B5012. Cross M6.

18 TL, SP Rugely (43km/27 miles), and climb gradually.

19 SO at XR, SP Rugeley/Cannock Chase Visitor Centre (views behind across Staffordshire, Shropshire and Welsh hills).

Enter Cannock Chase and climb Penkridge Bank.

20 For visitor centre, SO at XR and follow SP.

Otherwise, to follow main route, TL at XR, SP Cannock Chase German Military Cemetery.
40km (25 miles)

21 Pass German war cemetery on RHS. Climb and descend, with panoramic views on LHS. Pass tearooms on LHS (cyclists especially welcome).

22 TR, SP Car Park. Continue for descent to Brocton, looking out for fallow deer (and good views ahead).

23 TR by grass triangle and immediately TR at TJ, SP Rugeley. Enter Milford.

24 TR at mini roundabout, SP Rugeley. Immediately TL, SP Tixall. TL at TJ, SP Tixall (48km/30 miles). Cross railway, river and canal into Tixall.

25 TR at TJ, SP Great Haywood (ancient monument on LHS, folly on RHS, then Tixall Gatehouse on LHS, toll house RHS).

26 Keep R, SP Great Haywood. Cross river and canal and pass under railway.

27 TL at mini roundabout, no SP.

28 TL at TJ onto A51, SP Stone. TR, SP Stowe. Continue into Hixon.

29 TL at XR, SP Weston. *58km (36 miles)*

30 TL at TJ onto A518, SP Weston. Ruins on RHS are Chartley Castle (no public access).

31 Pass Amerton Farm on RHS. TR opposite Plough pub, no SP. Enjoy expansive views, particularly back towards Cannock Chase.

32 TR at TJ, no SP. **62km (38.5 miles)**

33 TL at TJ, SP Stone (64km/40 miles). Climb.

34 SO at XR, SP Stone. Good views on LHS. Climb and descend (more views).

35 TR at roundabout, SP Stone. Continue into Stone.

36 TL, SP Stafford. **73km (45.5 miles)**

37 To visit town centre, TR into Crown Street, SP Town Centre.

Otherwise, to follow main route, keep SO, SP Eccleshall. Cross River Trent and Trent and Mersey Canal.

38 SO at roundabout, SP Eccleshall. Cross M6.

39 TL at roundabout, SP Eccleshall.

40 To return to Norton Bridge railway station, TL.

To continue route, SO, across railway. Pass Bird of Prey Centre on LHS. **82km (51 miles)**

41 SO at mini roundabout, SP Loggerheads. Tearoom on LHS.

42 TL, SP Elford Heath. Climb.

43 TR at XR, SP Cop Mere. Continue towards Cop Mere.

44 SO at XR, SP Market Drayton. Pass mere on RHS. Continue through Bishop's Offley (pub on RHS open Wednesday–Sunday).

45 TL at XR, SP Shebdon (89km/55.5 miles). Continue for excellent views across to the Wrekin and the Stipperstones.

46 TR at XR, SP Newport.

47 SO at roundabout, SP Newport.

48 Enter Newport. TL at TJ, SP Town Centre B5082. TR into New Street and return to car park to finish the ride. **101km (63 miles)**

Places of interest along the route

Ⓐ Weston Park, Shifnal
The house was built in 1671 for the Earl of Bradford. It contains fine collections of art and antiques and is surrounded by over 405ha (1000 acres) of parkland. Restaurant. Open Easter to September – telelphone to confirm times. Charge. Telephone (01952) 852100; www.weston-park.com

Ⓑ Cannock Chase
The area was once the hunting ground of ancient royalty. Today Cannock Chase is a picturesque area of woodland walks, wildlife and superb scenery. See Route 16 for more details.

Ⓒ Tixall Gatehouse, Tixall
Standing alone in a field, the building comprises the stables and gatehouse of the long-vanished Tixall Hall, four storeys high and dating from 1598. No public access – the gatehouse is owned by the Landmark Trust who let it for holidays.

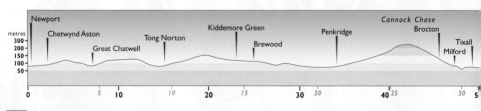

D Amerton Farm, Amerton

A working farm with a farm trail and lots of animals. Also narrow gauge railway, craft centre, bakery, pottery, dolls house shop, wildlife centre, puppet shop, garden centre, farm shop and tearoom. Open daily, April to September 0900–1800; October to March 0900–1700. Admission free. Telephone (01889) 270294; www.amertonfarm. com

E Bird of Prey Centre, Fletchers Country Garden Centre, Eccleshall

Captive bred birds are displayed here to raise money to help injured birds. Café in the garden centre. See Route 3 for more information.

Newport

Food and drink

Plenty of choice in Newport and various pubs and tearooms passed en route. Refreshments are also available at Weston Park, Amerton Farm and the Bird of Prey Centre.

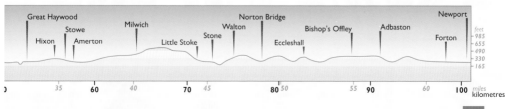

DROITWICH AND THE VALE OF EVESHAM

Route information

 Distance 106km (66 miles)

Grade Moderate

Terrain Mostly quiet roads, with some short stretches of busier A roads.

Time to allow 6–8 hours.

Getting there by car Droitwich is 9.5km (6 miles) north east of Worcester on the A38. There are several car parks in Droitwich. The route starts in the long stay car park, off Heritage Way and Saltway.

Getting there by train There is a railway station at Droitwich. For travel information telephone (08457) 484950 or visit www.nationalrail.co.uk

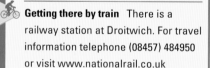

A ride in the countryside of Worcestershire and Warwickshire and through the Vale of Evesham. From Droitwich the route heads south as far as Eckington before turning east to Evesham. From here the route heads further east and then north as far as Alcester before turning west back to Droitwich.

Places of interest along the route

A Droitwich

A pleasant market town, centre for the salt industry since before Roman times. See Route 4 for more information.

B Vale of Evesham

The low-lying, fertile area of land which skirts the northern fringe of the Cotswold Hills between Evesham and Stratford-upon-Avon. It is a beautiful area and one of the most abundant fruit and vegetable growing areas in the country. The area is well-known for the beautiful displays of blossom each spring, usually between March and early May. **Evesham**, on the River Avon, is an ancient market town that grew up around **Evesham Abbey**, founded in the 8th century. The ruins can still be seen in the town centre. The **Almonry**, a 14th-century building, houses the Tourist Information Centre (TIC) and a Visitor Centre, containing much information on local history and an important collection of local artefacts. Also quiet garden. Open all year, Monday–Saturday 1000–1700, Sunday 1400–1700. Telephone the TIC for more information on (01386) 446944 or visit www.almonry.ndo.co.uk

C Domestic Fowl Trust, Honeybourne

The trust works in the conservation of rare and traditional farm animals and poultry. See Route 13 for more information.

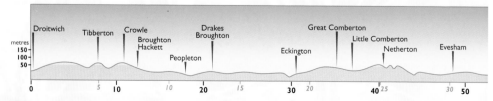

View to Bredon Hill

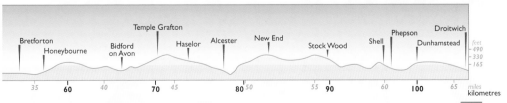

Bretforton Honeybourne Bidford on Avon Temple Grafton Haselor Alcester New End Stock Wood Shell Phepson Dunhamstead Droitwich

feet
490
330
165

35 60 40 70 45 80 50 55 90 60 100 65

miles
kilometres

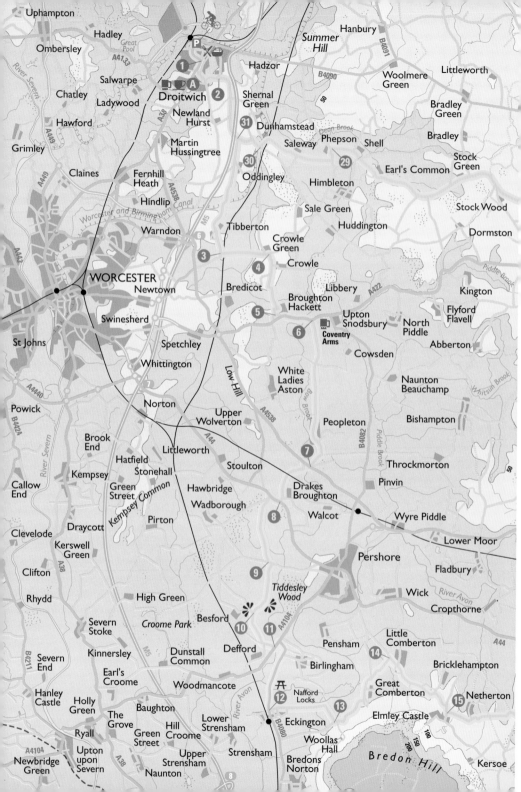

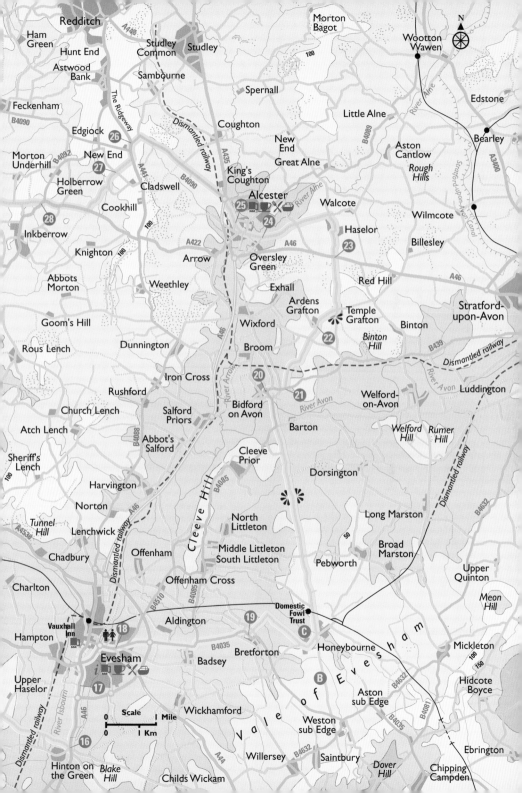

Route description

TR out of long stay car park (off Heritage Way and Saltway). TR at TJ and take first TR, no SP. TL at TJ into Saltway, no SP.

1 TR at mini roundabout into Worcester Road. TL into Tagwell Road, SP Oddingley.

2 Take first exit at roundabout, no SP. Continue under motorway, cross Worcester and Birmingham Canal and continue through Tibberton.

3 TL, SP Crowle. **8km (5 miles)**

4 TR, SP Broughton Hackett. Continue into Broughton Hackett.

5 TL at TJ, SP Alcester A422. TL at TJ, SP Stratford. Continue into Upton Snodsbury.

6 TR opposite Coventry Arms pub, SP Peopleton.

7 TR at TJ onto A4538, no SP (19km/ 12 miles). Immediately TL, SP Drakes Broughton.

8 TR at TJ, SP Worcester A44. Take first TL, SP Wadborough. Immediately TL, SP Defford.

9 TL at TJ, no SP. Immediately TR, SP Defford. **24km (15 miles)**

10 TL at TJ, SP Defford. Views of Bredon Hill and the Malverns.

11 TL at TJ, no SP. Immediately TR, SP Eckington B4080. Cross River Avon via Eckington Bridge (picnic site immediately on LHS). Continue into Eckington.

12 TL by cross in Eckington, SP Elmley Castle. Pass Nafford Locks on LHS.

13 TL at TJ, SP Comberton (33km/ 20.5 miles). Continue through Great Comberton.

14 TR at TJ, SP Elmley Castle. Continue into Elmley Castle.

15 TL by old cross, SP Evesham. **39.5km (24.5 miles)**

16 TL at TJ onto A46, SP Cheltenham. Take first exit at roundabout, SP Town Centre.

17 To visit town centre and riverside, SO at first set of traffic lights, at second set of traffic lights carry SO and cross River Avon or TR onto B4035 to continue route.

If visiting riverside TL by Vauxhall Inn opposite TIC. SP toilets SO at end of car park into Boat Lane. Follow lane to Hampton Ferry and River Avon passing café and restaurant on RHS. After visit retrace route and TL at traffic lights onto B4035.

18 TR at traffic lights, SP Broadway. Take second exit at roundabout, SP Badsey B4035. Continue towards Bretforton.

19 TL, SP Honeybourne (56km/35 miles). TL at XR in Honeybourne, SP Bidford on Avon. Domestic Fowl Trust is on L. Continue for panoramic views to Bidford on Avon. Pass park on LHS and cross River Avon.

20 Take third exit at roundabout, SP Stratford. **67.5km (42 miles)**

21 TL, SP Ardens Grafton. Continue and SO at XR, SP Ardens Grafton.

22 TR at TJ, SP Temple Grafton. Good views here. Continue into Temple Grafton. TL at XR, SP Alcester.

23 SO at XR across A46 (CARE), SP Great Alne (74km/46 miles). Pass through Haselor. TL at XR, SP Alcester.

24 TR at TJ, no SP. Enter Alcester. To visit town centre, TR into High Street.

Otherwise, to continue route, TL, no SP.

25 Take third exit at roundabout, SP Tourist Information. SO at traffic lights, no SP. Take second exit at roundabout, SP Droitwich (80.5km/50 miles). Climb to Ridgeway.

26 TL at TJ, SP Droitwich. TR into Wood Lane, no SP.

27 SO at XR, no SP. TR at TJ onto A422, no SP.

28 TR, SP Stockwood (88.5km/55 miles). SO at XR, SP Droitwich. Continue and cross ford via footbridge on LHS. *96.5km (60 miles)*

29 TL at TJ, SP Crowle. NB: next direction easy to miss! Take first TR, no SP. Cross railway and keep L.

30 TR at TJ, SP Droitwich. Cross canal and take first TL, SP Droitwich.

31 TR at TJ, SP Droitwich. Take third exit at roundabout, no SP. TR at TJ into Worcester Road, no SP, and retrace route back to car park to finish the ride. *106km (66 miles)*

Food and drink

Plenty of choice in Droitwich, Evesham and Alcester. Refreshments are also available at the Domestic Fowl Trust.

Eckington Bridge

WORCESTERSHIRE
24 – A GRANDE RANDONNÉE

Route information

🚲 **Distance** 107km (66.5 miles)

🚲 **Grade** Moderate

🚲 **Terrain** Quiet lanes and short stretches of busier A roads.

🚲 **Time to allow** 6–8 hours.

🚲 **Getting there by car** Droitwich is 9.5km (6 miles) north east of Worcester on the A38. There are several car parks in Droitwich. Use the one by St Andrews shopping centre/Victoria Square, close to the Tourist Information Centre (TIC) and the start of the route.

🚲 **Getting there by train** There is a railway station at Droitwich. For travel information telephone (08457) 484950 or visit www.nationalrail.co.uk

A route through the Worcestershire country-side. From the spa town of Droitwich the route heads west for a climb up Ankerdine Hill and views across Worcestershire to the Malvern Hills. On to Great Malvern and then Upton upon Severn, the southernmost point of the route. From here the route heads north back to Droitwich.

Route description

Start from Droitwich TIC and head west along Victoria Square. SO into Ombersley Street East which becomes Coleman Way. TL in Covercraft Lane.

1 SO at roundabout, SP Ombersley/Tenbury. Take third exit at next roundabout, SP Kidderminster.

2 TL at TJ, SP Kidderminser. Take third exit at roundabout, SP Kidderminster. Then take second exit at roundabout, SP Kidderminster. Continue into Hampton Lovett, ignoring first TL.

3 Take second TL, SP Doverdale. Continue SO at XR across A449, SP Lineholt.

8km (5 miles)

4 TL at XR, SP Boreley Holt Fleet. Good views!

5 TR at TJ, SP Holt Fleet. Keep R at grass triangle, no SP.

6 TL at TJ, no SP. TR at TJ onto A4133, no SP. Cross River Severn and climb. SO at XR, no SP.

7 TR at TJ, SP Tenbury A4133.

8 TL, SP Ockeridge. *16km (10 miles)*

9 SO at XR, SP Martley Wichenford.

10 TR, SP Martley. TL at XR, SP Martley. Continue into Martley.

11 TL at TJ onto B4204, no SP (shops on R in village). Continue on this road and climb Ankerdine Hill (viewing point and information board on L at top of hill). Descend hill. TL at foot of hill (CARE – sharp bend), SP Bromyard/Worcester.

12 TR at TJ, SP Leominster A44. Cross River Teme and TL, SP Suckley. Continue through Suckley.

13 TR at XR, SP Bromyard.

33.5km (21 miles)

14 TL (immediately before chapel), no SP.

15 TL at TJ (opposite Herefordshire House), SP Great Malvern B4219. TR, SP Stamford Bishop Church.

16 TL at TJ, no SP (40km/25 miles). Continue into Acton Beauchamp and SO at XR.

17 TL, SP Evesbatch. Descend into village.

18 TR at TJ, no SP.

19 TL at TJ onto A4103, no SP. Gradually climb.

20 TR at XR, no SP. Descend into Westfield.

21 SO at XR, SP Mathon (49.5km/31 miles). TR at TJ, SP Mathon, and continue through village.

22 TL (after village hall), SP West Malvern. Continue on this road for climb (steep near top) to West Malvern.

23 Keep L into Mathon Road, no SP. TL at TJ, no SP, and continue along edge of hill. Expansive views across Worcestershire on L. Pass Tank Quarry picnic site on RHS (58km/36 miles).

24 TR at TJ, SP Great Malvern, and continue into the town (café and two pubs on RHS).

25 TL (after Unicorn pub), SP Winter Gardens. Descend.

26 SO at green in road, SP Upton on Severn. Keep L, SP Welland B4208. TR, SP Welland B4208.

27 SO at XR, SP Gloucester (64km/40 miles). SO at XR, SP Upton upon Severn. Continue into the town.

28 TL at TJ, no SP (tearoom on corner). Keep R at roundabout, SP Pershore.

29 TL at TJ onto A38, no SP. Then take first TR, SP Pershore A4104 (73km/45.5 miles). Continue on this road.

30 TL by memorial, SP Croome Landscape Park.

31 TL, SP Kinnersley. Climb gradually for excellent views. TR, SP Croome/Croome Landscape Park. Continue under M5. Good views of Croome Hall on RHS and entrance to park.

32 TL at TJ, SP Wadborough (80.5km/50 miles). Follow this road into Wadborough.

33 TR, SP Defford.

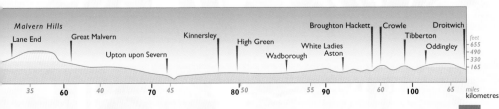

The Burf
Crossway Green
Norchard
Cutnall Green
Cooksey Corner
Stoke Heath
Stoke Pound
Tardebigge

Comhampton
Elmbridge
Broad Alley
Upton Warren
Stoke Prior
Banks Green
Woodgate

Lineholt
Dunhampton
Hampton Lovett
Wychbold
Sharpway Gate
Lower Bentley
Upper Bentley

Sytchampton
Doverdale
Rashwood
Astwood
Piper's Hill
Littleworth

Boreley
Uphampton
Hadley
Hanbury
Summer Hill
Woolmere Green
Bradley Green

Ombersley
Droitwich Spa
Hadzor
Bradley

Holt Fleet
A4133
Salwarpe
Droitwich
Shernal Green
Dunhamstead
Shell
Earl's Common

Holt Heath
Holt
Ladywood
Oddingley
Saleway
Phepson
Stock Green

Grimley
Hawford
Martin Hussingtree
Dunhamstead
Himbleton
Stock Wood

Sinton Green
Hallow Heath
Claines
Fernhill Heath
Sale Green
Huddington
Dormston

Shoulton
Hallow
Hindlip
Tibberton
Crowle Green

Peachley
Warndon
Crowle
Libbery
Kington

Lower Broadheath
WORCESTER
Newtown
Broughton Hackett
Flyford Flavell

Upper Broadheath
Henwick
Swinesherd
Spetchley
Upton Snodsbury
North Piddle
Abberton

St Johns
Rushwick
Whittington
Churchill
Cowsden

Kings End
Norton
White Ladies Aston
Naunton Beauchamp
Bishampton

Collett's Green
Powick
Upper Wolverton
Peopleton

Bastonford
Callow End
Brook End
Littleworth
Stoulton
Throckmorton
Pinvin

Deblin's Green
Kempsey
Hatfield
Stonehall
Hawbridge
Plough and Harrow
Drakes Broughton
Walcot
Wyre Piddle

Draycott
Green Street
Wadborough
Lower Moor

Clevelode
Kerswell Green
Pirton
Fladbury

Clifton
High Green
Pershore
Tiddesley Wood
Wick
Cropthorne

Guarlford
Rhydd
Besford
Pensham
Little Comberton

Hanley Swan
Croome Park
Kinnersley
Defford
Birlingham
Bricklehampton

Severn Stoke
Dunstall Common
Woodmancote
Eckington
Great Comberton
Netherton

Brotheridge Green
Severn End
Baughton
The Grove
Lower Strensham
Elmley Castle
Kersoe

Holly Green
Naunton
Strensham
Bredon Hill

Upton upon Severn

Dismantled railway

River Severn
River Teme
River Avon
Worcester and Birmingham Canal
Kempsey Common

34 TL at TJ onto A44, SP Worcester. Pass Plough and Harrow pub. TR, SP Droitwich B4084.

35 TL at TJ, no SP (90km/56 miles). TR, SP White Ladies. Continue through White Ladies.

36 TR at TJ, SP Churchill/Broughton Hackett. Cycle through Churchill to junction with A422.

37 TR at TJ, SP Stratford A422. Immediately TL, SP Crowle/Tibberton. TR, SP Crowle, and continue into Crowle.

38 TL at TJ, SP Droitwich. *96.5km (60 miles)*

39 TR at TJ, SP Droitwich. Pass through Tibberton and Oddingley, under M5 towards outskirts of Droitwich.

40 Take third exit at roundabout, no SP. Descend (Tagwell Road). TR at TJ into Worcester Road. Descend to mini roundabout where SO. TL into St Andrews and finish ride by TIC. *107km (66.5 miles)*

Places of interest along the route

Ⓐ Droitwich Spa

Droitwich is a pleasant market town and has been a centre for the salt industry since before Roman times. See Route 4 for further information.

Ⓑ Great Malvern

The town sits on the steep east slope of the Malvern Hills. The **Priory Church**, Church Street, was founded in the 11th century as a monastery. Although the exterior is mainly 15th- and 16th-century, the interior contains many original Norman features including wall tiles and a large window containing medieval glass. Picnic area. Open daily, April to October 0900–1830; November to March 0900–1630. Admission free. Telephone (01684) 561020. **Malvern Museum**, Abbey Road, is situated in the priory gatehouse, the medieval gatehouse

to the monastery, and describes local geology and local history through the ages. Open April to October, daily 1030–1700. Small charge. Contact the TIC for more information on (01684) 892289 or visit www.malvern-spa.u-net.com

Ⓒ Upton upon Severn

The town is situated on the River Severn and contains many old timbered and early Georgian buildings. The highly visible 13th-century tower and 18th-century copper-covered cupola are all that remain of a church that was demolished in 1937. The **Pepperpot**, Church Street, is a heritage centre describing the town's history, its part in the Civil War and its links with the river. Open Easter to September, telephone to confirm times on (01684) 592679. The **Tudor House**, Church Street, contains lots of local artifacts. Open April to October, daily 1400–1700; winter weekends only. Telephone (01684) 592447. Contact the TIC for more information on the town on (01684) 594200 or visit www.upton.uk.net

Ⓓ Croome Park, Severn Stoke

The park was Capability Brown's first complete landscape. The National Trust is undertaking a long-term restoration plan, but there is plenty for visitors to see now, including the lakeside garden, grotto and wilderness walk. Kiosk sells soft and ice cream. Picnic area. Open 1100–1700: April and October, weekends and bank holidays; May to September, Friday–Monday. Charge. Telephone (01905) 371006 or visit www.nationaltrust.org.uk

Food and drink

There is plenty of choice in Droitwich, Great Malvern and Upton upon Severn. Martley has a convenience store.

Ⓟ **Plough and Harrow, near Pershore**
Open all day, every day.

SHROPSHIRE – A GRANDE RANDONNÉE

Route information

 Distance   113.5km (70.5 miles)

 Grade   Moderate

Terrain   Quiet lanes and B roads, and short sections of busier A roads.

Time to allow   6–9 hours.

Getting there by car   Ironbridge is 4.5km (3 miles) south of Dawley on the B4373, close to the A4169 and A442. Park in the Bridge long stay car park on the B4373.

Getting there by train   The easiest railway access is from Craven Arms. For travel information telephone (08457) 484950 or visit www.nationalrail.co.uk

A tour around unspoilt and sparsely populated Shropshire. The route starts from Ironbridge, the cradle of the industrial revolution, and heads south west through Much Wenlock almost as far as Craven Arms. From here the route turns south east through Ludlow to Tenbury Wells. Here the route turns north for the return to Ironbridge, via Bridgnorth. The route follows a short section of the National Cycle Network (NCR 81). This route would make a good two day tour – start at Craven Arms and stay overnight in Ironbridge (Ironbridge Youth Hostel telephone (01952) 588755; Woodbridge Inn, Ironbridge telephone (01952) 882054).

Places of interest along the route

Ⓐ Ironbridge

The World Heritage site at Ironbridge Gorge marks the building of the world's first cast iron bridge, constructed to span the River Severn and an important part of the Industrial Revolution. See Route 6 for more details.

Ⓑ Benthall Hall, Broseley

An impressive stone house with gardens. For more details on the hall and Broseley town, see Route 18.

Ⓒ Wenlock Priory, Much Wenlock

The substantial remains of a priory, with 12th-century carvings, lawns and ornamental topiary. See Route 18 for more details.

Ⓓ Ludlow

A small town on the hill about the River Teme, well-known for its festival held each June. Craft and food fairs are also held during the year. **Ludlow Castle** was built in the late 11th century and features medieval and Tudor architecture. Open daily, February to April and October to December, 1000–1600; May to September, 1000–1700. Charge. Telephone (01584) 873355. Below the castle is **Linney Riverside Park**, with picnic area, children's playground and rowing boats for hire May to September. **Castle Lodge**, of medieval origin, was home to the officials of the Council of the Marches. It is open to the public. The **Parish Church** was rebuilt during the 15th century and contains fine stained glass. There is a memorial to A E Houseman, author of *A Shropshire Lad*, in the churchyard. Stewards are on duty spring, summer and autumn. Open all year, daily 1000–1700.

Bridgnorth

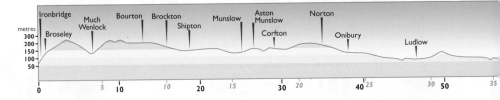

metres
300
200
150
100
50

Ironbridge
Broseley
Much
Wenlock
Bourton
Brockton
Shipton
Munslow
Aston
Munslow
Corfton
Norton
Onibury
Ludlow

0   5   10   10   20   15   30 20   40 25   30 50   35

Donation requested. Telephone (01584) 872073 for information. **Ludlow Museum** describes the town's history, from the building of the castle to the present day. Telephone the Tourist Information Centre for more information on (01584) 875053 or visit www.ludlow.org.uk

ⓔ Severn Valley Railway, Highley
The railway offers a 25.5km (16 mile) journey along the Severn Valley, from Bridgnorth to Highley and on to Bewdley and Kidderminster. See Route 18 for more details.

ⓕ Severn Valley Country Park, Highley
The country park comprises a large area of the Severn Valley. See Route 18 for more details.

ⓖ Bridgnorth
The town is split into the High Town (town centre) on the cliff top and the Low Town across the River Severn. A cable railway connects the two. See Route 18 for more information.

Route description

To start from Craven Arms railway station, exit station and TL to junction with A49. SO (CARE) A49 and follow B4368 to pick up route at direction 6, where TR, SP Norton.

To start from Ironbridge (at the southern end of the bridge by the tollhouse), TR at TJ, no SP, and climb.

1 TR at TJ, SP Much Wenlock. Continue, passing Benthall Hall on RHS.

2 TR, SP Much Wenlock. Descend to Much Wenlock (priory ruins in R in town centre).

3 TL into Queens Street (opposite priory entrance). Take first TL, no SP. Then TR at TJ, no SP.

4 TR at TJ into A458. Immediately TL, SP Craven Arms B4378 (8km/5 miles).

5 TR at TJ, SP Craven Arms (30.5km/ 19 miles). Continue along B4368 through Munslow and Aston Munslow towards Craven Arms.

6 To return to Craven Arms railway station, SO at XR and retrace route to station to finish the ride.

Otherwise, to follow main route, TL at XR, SP Norton.

7 Keep R, SP Onibury. Descend into Onibury. TL at TJ, SP Walton (shop and café on LHS).

8 TL at TJ, no SP (40km/25miles). Cycle through golf course and race course. TR at TJ, no SP.

9 TL at TJ onto A49, SP Leominster. Take first TL, SP Ludlow B4361. Continue into Ludlow.

10 Keep R, SP Town Centre. In town centre, climb SO at XR (45km/28 miles). To visit Ludow Castle or church, TR, SP Castle.

Otherwise, continue through town and descend.

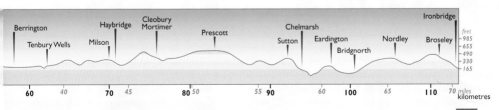

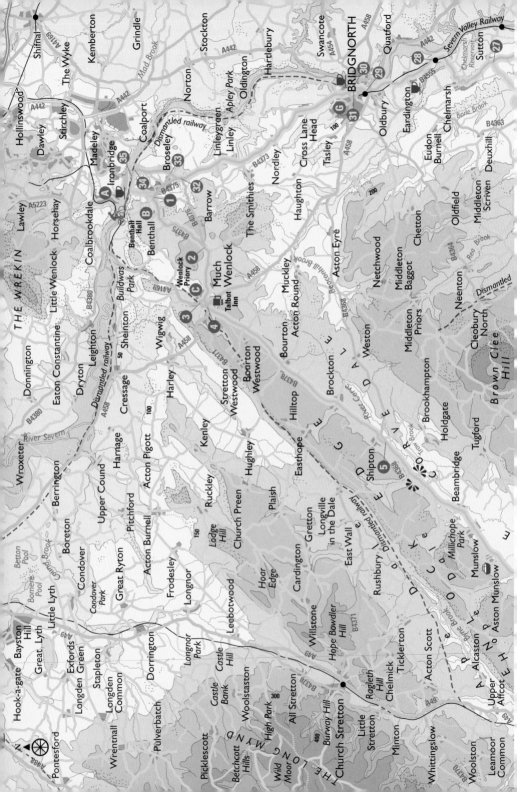

11 TL, SP Kidderminster. TR by old toll house, no SP. Cycling alongside River Teme.

12 TR at TJ into Steventon New Road, no SP.

13 SO at XR, SP Tenbury.

49km (30.5 miles)

14 TR, SP Little Hereford.

15 TR at TJ onto A456, SP Brimfield. Cross river and take first TL, SP Leysters.

16 Take first TL, SP Berrington.

17 TL at grass triangle, SP Tenbury (58km/36 miles). Continue into Tenbury Wells.

18 TL at TJ, no SP. Continue through Tenbury. Cross River Teme.

19 TL at TJ, SP Ludlow A456. Take first TR, SP Cleobury Mortimer. Continue along this undulating road and descend to Cleobury Mortimer.

20 TR at TJ onto A4117, no SP. Descend.

21 TL, SP Highley B4363.

72.5km (45 miles)

22 TL at XR, SP Bagginswood.

23 Keep R, SP Bagginswood.

24 TL at TJ, SP Oreton. Take first TR, SP Billingsley (81km/50.5 miles). Continue SO at XR, SP Billingsley.

25 TR at TJ, SP Chorley. Continue into Billingsley.

26 TL at TJ, SP Chelmarsh B4363. Take first TR into Covert Lane, no SP.

27 Pass TR to Severn Valley Railway and Country Park. TL at TJ onto B4555, no SP.

89km (55.5 miles)

28 Pass café on LHS and continue on B4555 into Bridgnorth.

29 TR at TJ, SP Town Centre (97.5km/ 60.5 miles). Almost immediately TR at TJ, SP Stourbridge.

30 TL (before bridge over River Severn) into Under Hill Street. Keep L into Cartway (NB: this is one-way street SP No Entry – walk up). Keep L, SP Hightown. Continue uphill into town centre.

31 TR at TJ (road will shortly become two-way). Pass through Northgate Arch. Continue along B4373 towards Ironbridge.

32 Keep SO, SP Ironbridge.

108.5km (67.5 miles)

33 Keep R, SP Ironbridge. Descend and keep R, SP Ironbridge Museums.

34 TR (before bridge over River Severn), SP Tile Centre/Maws Craft Centre.

35 TR by disused level crossing, SP Cycle Route 81 (Jackfield Sidings). Continue along cycleway into car park. Follow SP Cycle Route to end of Ironbridge, by tollhouse, to finish the ride.

113.5km (70.5 miles)

Food and drink

Plenty of choice in Ironbridge, Tenbury Wells, Ludlow, Bridgnorth and Cleobury Mortimer.

Talbot Inn, Much Wenlock
Free house. Snacks and meals.

CTC
(Cyclists' Touring Club)

working for cycling

CTC is the UK's national cycling organisation. With seventy thousand members and affiliates, the club works for all twenty-two million cyclists in England, Wales, Scotland and Northern Ireland. CTC successfully lobbies on behalf of all cyclists and helped the government create its National Cycling Strategy. CTC also campaigns for improved countryside access, better cycling facilities on roads and at the workplace, and more space for bikes on public transport.

CTC provides essential services and invaluable advice for novice and experienced cyclists of all ages and abilities. It has 64 District Associations with 204 local groups plus hundreds of local campaigners in its Right to Ride network. New members and volunteers are always welcomed!

Cyclecover Insurance Services

CTC membership includes free third party insurance and legal aid. CTC also offers several cycling-specific insurance policies. Cyclecover Rescue is a unique twenty-four hour rescue scheme for cyclists stranded by breakdown (excluding punctures), accident, vandalism or theft. CTC offers annual travel insurance and single trip cover. Mountain biking, touring, repatriation of bike, luggage and accessory cover are all included. Comprehensive cycle insurance is offered to members and non-members alike, at very competitive premiums.

CycleSafe

Local authorities are being urged to sign up to four CycleSafe objectives, the aims of which are to improve safety for cyclists. That means reducing risks on roads, consideration for cyclists in new road layouts, adequate investment in cycling facilities and in cycling promotion. CTC has offered all authorities advice on engineering measures, education and examples of successful schemes elsewhere. In York, Britain's most cycling-friendly city, the implementation of a comfortable cycling environment has increased cycling by sixteen per cent and led to a ten per cent drop in cycling casualties in the last 20 years.

Technical and Touring Advice

CTC offers advice on buying a bike and other cycling equipment, maintenance and repair. CTC's events department has information on hundreds of routes both in the UK and abroad and experienced leaders run holidays to scores of destinations throughout the world. These tours are suitable for all cyclists ranging from families with young children to experienced distance riders.

CTC Magazine

Cycle Touring and Campaigning is CTC's bi-monthly magazine which is free to members. Articles cover campaign news, tours, technical advice, event reports and equipment tests.

CTC Help Desk

Staff on the Help Desk answer queries on all things cycling, from contacts at your local group to the best route across the continent. The Help Desk can advise on travelling by train or bus with your bike, bike security and parking facilities in public places and on how to make the workplace more friendly to cyclists.

CTC Membership

Membership costs from just £10 per year. Whether you are a roadster, prefer the quiet of canal paths and the countryside, commute by bike or just enjoy a day out with the children, CTC is the essential accessory for you!

For more information contact the CTC Help Desk:
CTC, 69 Meadrow, Godalming, Surrey GU7 3HS
Telephone 0870 873 0060
Email cycling@ctc.org.uk
Website www.ctc.org.uk

Cyclecover Travel Insurance
For a quote or instant cover:
Telephone 0870 873 0068
Visit www.cyclecover.co.uk

Cyclecover Rescue
Telephone free on 0800 212810.

Cyclecover Cycle Insurance
Telephone free on 0800 169 5798.

CycleSafe
Visit www.cyclesafe.org.uk